Contemporary
sociology of
the school
General editor
JOHN EGGLESTON

Schooling in rural societies

CONTEMPORARY SOCIOLOGY
OF THE SCHOOL

ROY NASH

Schooling
in
rural
societies

METHUEN

First published in 1980 by
Methuen & Co. Ltd
11 New Fetter Lane, London EC4P 4EE
Published in the USA by
Methuen & Co.
in association with Methuen, Inc.
733 Third Avenue, New York, NY 10017
© 1980 Roy Nash
Typeset by Inforum Ltd, Portsmouth
Printed in the United States of America

British Library Cataloguing in Publication Data
Nash, Roy
Schooling in rural societies. — (Contemporary
sociology of the school).
1. Education, Rural
2. Educational sociology
I. Title   II. Series
301.5'6   LC5146   79-41819
ISBN 0-416-73300-X
ISBN 0-416-73310-7 Pbk

CONTENTS

Acknowledgements

A book which cuts across so many academic disciplines as this could not have been written without an immense amount of co-operation from others. My former colleagues who worked with me in the Rural Education Research Unit, Department of Education, Bangor – Howard Williams, Marisse Evans and Catrin Roberts – ought to be mentioned first. Several others at Bangor, Professor J. R. Webster who made it possible for me to write in a busy teaching department, Glyn Williams who made me welcome in the sociology of Wales group, and Colin Terry who let me know what was happening in the field of independent learning, were particularly helpful. The Interskola Conferences at Bangor Normal and Keswick Hall Colleges of Education were an invaluable source of information and I trust that the friends I made there will understand that my absence from their meetings in the next few years will not be due to lack of interest. Thanks also to Michael Montgomery who lent me several otherwise unobtainable papers on recent developments in Nigerian education.

The manuscript was completed after my removal to Massey

University, New Zealand, and I know that the typists there who worked there on the various drafts, Frances Crawford and Naomi Weblock, would like to see their names in print: many thanks.

Finally, the publishers and I would like to thank Penguin Books Ltd for permission to reproduce the extract on pp. 55–6.

Editor's introduction

Sociology has changed dramatically in the past decade. Sociologists have provided an ever increasing diversity of empirical and theoretical approaches that are advancing our understanding of the complexities of societies and their educational arrangements. It is now possible to see the over-simplification of the earlier sociological view of the world running smoothly with agreed norms of behaviour, with institutions and individuals performing functions that maintained society and where even conflict was restricted to 'agreed' areas. This normative view of society with its functionalist and conflict theories has now been augmented by a range of interpretative approaches in which the realities of human interaction have been explored by phenomenologists, ethnomethodologists and other reflexive theorists. Together they have emphasized the part that individual perceptions play in determining social reality and have challenged many of the characteristics of society that the earlier sociologists had assumed to be 'given'.

The new approaches have had striking effects upon the sociology of the school. Earlier work was characterized by a range of incompletely examined assumptions about such matters as ability, opportunity and social class. Sociologists asked how working-class children could achieve in the schools like middle-class children. Now they also ask how a social system defines class, opportunities and achievement. Such concepts and many other such as subjects, the curriculum and even schools themselves are seen to be products of the social system in which they exist. In our study of the school we can now explore more fully the ways in which individual teachers' and students' definitions of their situation help to determine its social arrangements; how perceptions of achievement can not only define achievement but also identify those who achieve; how expectations about schooling can determine the very nature and evaluation of schools.

This series of volumes explores the main areas of the sociology of the school in which new understanding of events is now available. Each introduces the reader to the new interpretations, juxtaposes them against the longer standing perspectives and re-appraises the contemporary practice of education and its consequences.

In each, specialist authors develop their own analyses of central issues such as poverty, opportunity, comprehensive schooling, the language and interaction of the classroom, the teacher's role, the ecology of education, and ways in which education acts as an instrument of social control. The broad spectrum of themes and treatments is closely interrelated; it is offered to all who seek new illumination on the practice of education and to those who wish to know how contemporary sociological theory can be applied to educational issues.

In recent years sociologists have paid most attention to urban education, particularly to schooling in the inner city. Their studies have shown a clear connection between the community environment and the activities of schools and classrooms. Yet by far the majority of the world's children live and go to school in a rural context; this is the case even for many of the most 'developed' countries. In this volume Roy Nash demonstrates that the relationship between environment and schooling is equally strong in the rural areas and assembles extensive evidence from the developed and the less developed world to illustrate the strong and distinctive characteristics to which this gives rise in the rural schools.

The book makes it clear that most of the important areas of sociological concern in education are to be found in the rural schools. There is a full exploration of the less visible, but often more total, ways in which opportunity and achievement may be determined in the rural schools showing that they too may act as powerful agents of social control. With the aid of recent research reports, the book illustrates areas of disadvantage, linguistic usage and ethnic differentiation that are at least as significant as those to be found in the urban schools.

In his wide-ranging and comprehensive analysis, Roy Nash throws a new light on rural education that will be of major importance to those who seek a clearer perspective on the work of both rural and urban schools in contemporary societies.

John Eggleston

1

Sociology and
rural life

In Britain about $8\frac{1}{2}$ million people, or 17 per cent of the total, live in the rural regions. Even when those living in cities and towns with more than 7000 inhabitants are excluded there still remain more than $4\frac{1}{2}$ million in small towns and villages. And yet Britain is one of the world's most urbanized countries. In many parts of Europe the rural population makes up an even greater proportion of the population and, even where the proportion may be less, as in Scandinavia, the problems of remoteness are often greater. The rural areas are particularly significant in many parts of what used to be known as the New World – North America and Australasia. In the less developed countries of Asia, Africa and Latin America the rural population are the majority and their development is crucial to the progress of those continents.

Yet, because of the dominance of the urban centres, the problems associated with schooling in rural areas are a relatively neglected field of research. Indeed, even the term 'rural education', in the sense it will be used in this book, may not be understood without explanation. Here it will mean the study of the problems of education in rural societies. It thus has an exactly parallel meaning to the term 'urban education'. But it has also been used to mean the teaching of rural subjects, for example, gardening and natural history. In these pages these subjects will be called 'rural studies'.

This book thus opens up new ground. Consequently, I have thought it appropriate to discuss the issues from as broad a standpoint as possible. It will largely be concerned with Britain, and within Britain to a considerable extent with Wales, not only because all my empirical research in rural education has been carried out in Wales but because Wales developed a pattern of rural education markedly different from its powerful neighbour and provides an exceptionally good example of many of the major themes. It will also be concerned with developments in Europe, particularly in Scandinavia where a significant policy shift is taking place in rural education, and with the less developed countries which face a different challenge.

So far the word 'rural' has been left undefined. The 'rural regions' mentioned in the first sentence refer to the standard UK planning regions and are obviously concepts of economic geography. 'Rural' and 'urban' are geographical terms. How they came to have a sociological referent is an interesting story.

Rural sociology

There is nothing that can be called a sociology of rural education, as I have implied, but there is a rural sociology and it is helpful to be familiar with its concerns. The genesis of rural sociology can be found in the agricultural depression which hit the USA and Europe during the 1890s. The first course seems to have been taught in Chicago in 1894–5. The subject spread across the Mid-western states through the Land Grant Colleges which had been established to provide education and training for the farmers of the recently settled plains. The early writers were concerned with the problems of their time and place: with the farming family, the location of settlements, the supply of seasonal labour, the assimilation of immigrants and so on. The subject owed little to theoretical developments in sociology and the analyses remained at a low level. The immediate problems were solved by the recovery of agriculture before 1910 and the subject made little progress until the 1930s. Once again the stimulus was depression. In 1934 more than $1\frac{1}{2}$ million farming families were receiving welfare relief and substantial federal funds went into surveys and policy-oriented studies. It was during these years that rural sociology became professionally organized, a point marked by the establishment in 1936 of the *Rural Sociology Journal*. The major textbook of the time by Sorokin and Zimmerman (1929) is still read and their massive three volume *Source Book* was reprinted as recently as 1960. The conceptual breakthrough which they contributed lay in the systematic comparison of rural and urban culture and life style. The differences between urban and rural life were compared and contrasted and it was taken for granted that the geographical and economic distinction between urban and rural had a sociological significance. Later textbooks, for example, Smith and Zopf (1970), emphasized the continuum between rural and urban living and were a little less dogmatic about the necessary conditions of rural existence. Nevertheless, this tradition of rural sociology is so deeply rooted in its Mid-western origins that it is difficult to relate its concerns to other societies and its alarming ethnocentricity has been recognized as a fault so crippling that little further progress is likely to be made within this paradigm.

In Britain, sociologists who have been interested in rural societies have gained their inspiration from a different American tradition – that of community studies. The Middletown community studies of the Lynds (1929, 1937) and of Warner and his colleagues (1963), whose studies of Yankee City fill five volumes, had a direct influence on community sociologists working in Britain. Some of the British studies are usefully summarized and compared in Frankenberg (1966), although at least two major studies by Emmett (1964) and Littlejohn (1963) are omitted. Bell and Newby's (1974) collection of British and American community studies is also an important source. The concept of community has no necessary relationship to rurality and it is to some extent a matter of chance that so many British studies have been of small rural communities. It may have been the small size of these communities, which made them seemingly easier to study by a single researcher with limited time, rather than their location in the countryside which made them attractive. Despite the contingent relationship between rurality and community, rurally situated community studies not only dominate rural sociology but are now all but synonymous with it.

Rural-urban differences

In the popular imagination the rural world is seen as slow-moving and out-of-touch with progressive social movements, idyllic perhaps, but dull. This conventional view is not far removed from that of rural sociology – a view which can be traced back to Ferdinand Tonnies. Tonnies (1957) saw rural life characterized by associations of kinship (blood), friendship (mind) and neighbourliness (land), where a man's standing in his community was defined by his place in a traditional hierarchy. Rural society was, therefore, stable, intimate and resistant to outside influences. Urban life, by contrast, was seen as characterized by rational contract between men unconnected by traditional ties, and thus dynamic and open to change. The German terms *gesellschaft* and *gemeinschaft* are still in common use to describe, respectively, these distinguishing features of rural and urban life. Successive writers have drawn attention to various aspects of this dichotomy: Durkheim's (1972) mechanical as opposed to organic solidarity, Redfield's (1968) 'urban' and 'folk' modes of thought and Smith and Zopf's (1970) inductive typology of rural–urban differences are probably the most widely accepted.

Smith and Zopf's work, as the most recent formulation of an old theme, is worth examining in some detail. They state that rural societies differ from urban in the following eight respects: in the narrower pattern of occupations; in the smaller size of the community; in the lower density of the population; in the higher quality of the physical environment; in having less complex social differentiation and less well-defined social stratification; in having fewer opportunities for social mobility; in having a smaller social world and in having greater social solidarity.

This is a clear statement of what was the dominant view until the mid-1960s when a growing dissatisfaction with these con-

14

cepts was brought to a head in a seminal paper by Pahl (1966). As an introduction to his argument, and as a way of understanding why dissatisfaction with the conventional view had become so great, consider Smith and Zopf's list in relation to two Welsh communities as they were during the decades around the turn of the century, at the time when Tonnies was writing.

If we had examined the town of Llanelli in South Wales and the village of Trefor in Caernarvonshire we would have found that the range of occupations was almost as great in Trefor (farming, quarrying, services) as in Llanelli (mining, tin plate manufacture, services). The size of the communities was certainly different but it has to be shown that this has anything more than a geographical significance. Again the density of the population was greater in Llanelli than in Trefor but the sociological relevance of this is unclear (the people in the close-packed terraced houses of Llanelli and in the huddle of cottages in the centre of Trefor must have had the same experience of crowdedness). The quality of the physical environment is a complex variable to measure but the notion that, in these terms, life in the countryside is preferable to life in the town, is difficult to support on any rational grounds. The extent of social differentiation was essentially the same in Llanelli and in Trefor (the English speaking aristo-gentry landowner/capitalist class at the top and the Welsh speaking labouring class at the bottom). Opportunities for social mobility were scarce in both communities but there was probably a greater chance of social mobility through education in Trefor than in Llanelli. It is not at all clear that the social world of the village was smaller than the social world of the town (it would have needed a comparative study of the social networks of the two communities to resolve the question satisfactorily) and as for social solidarity, there was very little sense of there being one community either in Trefor or in Llanelli. In the village the major struggle was between the landowners and their tenants and between them and the impoverished labourers. In Llanelli the struggle was against the worst abuses of capitalist employment and certainly led to intense feelings of social solidarity and the development of a political movement amongst the great majority of the working people. If they are counted as the real community then community solidarity was greater in the town than in the village.

The argument is not that there were no differences between the industrial town of Llanelli and the semi-industrialized village of Trefor but that these differences had little to do with their urban and rural location and that an analysis of those communities in terms of *gesellschaft* and *gemeinschaft* would have positively obscured the fundamental similarities between them.

Pahl argues that the rural–urban continuum has little significance for sociologists by drawing attention to counterfactual cases. First, there are the 'urban villages' which exist within the confines of large cities. The best known example to British sociologists is Young and Willmott's (1962) study of family life in Bethnal Green in the East End of London which shows that community (*gesellschaftlich*) features are not untypical of city life. Secondly, Pahl's (1964) own studies of commuter villages in Hertfordshire strongly suggest that class and life cycle stage are the most significant variables in the explanation of the social groupings in those villages. The theoretically expected community features are not found. It is true that the small size of the villages offers the opportunity to learn about the life styles of classes which would be more remote in the city and the possibility of participating in a more integrated pattern of relationships may be one of the reasons why professional class commuters chose to live there. But, in objective terms, the differences between village suburbs and city fringe suburbs are minimal.

So far the argument has been essentially negative. It has been concerned to refute the too ready association of *place* of living with *style* of living. Put like that it may not seem that any such refutation is needed but so long as influential policy makers believe that there is a necessary association the argument has to be made. Such a belief is still deeply ingrained in many administrators. Garvey (1976) quotes Spreadbury, a senior official of Cambridgeshire LEA:

> The danger of vegetating in a backwater is almost inevitable. It is hard for a teacher to provide the opportunities for stimulus and change. In the urban school problems press in from all sides, but in the village, life is remote, irresponsible,

problem free. Travel is difficult, village children can remain educationally and socially stranded, with few facilities to compensate and no competition to spur them on.

In a vulgarized form this is Tonnies' view.

If Pahl's criticisms are accepted, if rural areas are no longer seen as giving rise to distinct patterns of life, then what are sociologists with an interest in rural areas to do? If there are no differences between rural and urban life, why study rural life in the first place?

A new perspective

The purpose of sociologists working in the rural areas is, according to Pahl, to study the integration of the rural population into the regional and national economic and social system. The meaningful distinction is thus not between urban and rural life styles but between local and national needs. The local and the national confront each other in the urban as much as in the rural physical setting; it is not the spatial aspect but the temporal process which is important. He writes:

> Neither the physical characteristics of the settlement nor the occupational structure of the population in themselves lead to social change – that is either fundamental changes in an individual's behaviour to others and their behaviour to him and/or broader, more fundamental, changes in the structure of society, for example in its economic or political system.

This implies that the differences between urban and rural life, in developed countries at least, are caused by:

1 Low population densities and small settlement size (the demographic and geographical definitions of rurality) which give rise to problems in the provision of services including education, and
2 A confrontation between national and local needs which has led to the decline of remote communities and created obvious difficulties.

This latter point is made forcibly by Day (1977) writing in the context of Wales:

17

. . . the everyday concerns of people in Mid-Wales – depopulation, decay of social provision, tourism, second homes, the struggle to preserve a language – do not find straightforward correspondence in the valleys and cities of South Wales, or on Deeside, where issues of decision making in nationalized industries, the role of multi-nationals and large scale impact of capital, urbanization and suburbanization, bulk larger.

These concerns are not related to differences in *gesellschaft* and *gemeinschaft* but to a particular stage in the long confrontation between the powerful centre and the weaker periphery.

It is the position taken in this introduction that the problems of rural education are not different in kind from those in urban areas, and are certainly not brought about by any supposedly necessary characteristics of rural life, but are to be understood as determined by the relationships which exist between the urban centres and the rural areas. Chapter 2 discusses how rural education has been dominated by conflicting demands for an education related to the local economy and for one which provides access to high status academic knowledge. Educational disadvantage is typically associated with the inner cities but it has been increasingly realized that a significant number of rural children can also be regarded as disadvantaged on the criteria normally used. This is discussed in chapter 3. Rural primary education is still based on the pattern established in the latter part of the nineteenth century. The official reports regard the smallest schools as educationally inefficient and uneconomic and have recommended their amalgamation with larger schools. Organized opposition to these proposals is affecting the process of local decision-making and forms the theme of chapter 4.

The current crisis of the village school has been precipitated by the reduction in family size which has produced a decline in primary school enrolments and will, in a predictably short time, begin to affect the secondary schools. The effectiveness of small schools and some of the strategies that might be adopted to improve it are discussed in chapter 5. It is no accident that the old ethnic and linguistic minorities in Britain, the Welsh and the Scottish Gaels, retain their community strength only in remote rural areas. The educational provision for these minorities is not only worth studying in its own right but may have implications for the education of newly arrived ethnic minorities. This will be discussed in chapter 6. Although there has been astonishingly little recognition of the special problems of rural education there have been a number of initiatives in recent years, both in Britain and overseas, designed to support teachers working in small and remote schools. These are the subject of chapter 7. Rural education will always be a matter of secondary importance in the urban, industrialized countries. But in the less developed countries it is likely to be essential to their continued social and economic progress. Chapter 8 is intended to be an introduction to the main issues in this complex and major problem. The relationship between the urban centres and the rural periphery are managed by the policies of regional economists and town and country planners. The argument outlined above about the task of rural sociologists will be further developed in relation to their work in the final chapter.

In summary, these are the concerns of rural education and of this book.

2

Themes in
rural education

A central and persistent theme in rural education can be found in the tension between the demands for education in locally relevant knowledge and in nationally relevant knowledge. In practice this tension is realized in the demand and provision for courses leading to work in the industries of the locality and for courses leading to qualifications offering the opportunity for social and geographical mobility. The attempt of the Scottish Society for Promoting Christian Knowledge spinning schools to provide a rural curriculum, with the aim of strengthening the economic base of rural society, is contrasted with the liberal curriculum of the Cambridgeshire village colleges, which had as their aim the strengthening of the cultural and community base of rural society. These two paradigm cases provide an introduction to the discussion of the selective function of rural education in Britain with particular reference to the case of Wales.

An experiment in rural education

The story of the SSPCK spinning schools is not widely known but it provides a most useful example of how an educational system can be constructed for community development. The SSPCK gained its first charter to establish schools to combat 'ignorance and barbarism' in the Scottish highlands in 1709, two years after the Act of Union. Mason (1936) shows that by 1715 there were twenty-five schools teaching writing, reading, English (not Gaelic), arithmetic and Church music. By 1732 the number of schoolmasters had grown to 109 and the SSPCK sought a new charter to provide instruction in 'some of the most useful and necessary arts of life' including spinning, weaving, knitting, agriculture and manufactures. Under the second charter awarded in 1738 the first farm school with forty acres was established at Grenock and, although the school failed, it stimulated the SSPCK to gain the co-operation of the Board of Manufactures to establish a number of industrial schools. After the 1745 rising, great tracts of highland land were seized by the Crown and placed under the control of the Commissioners for Managing the Forfeited Estates in Scotland whose policy was to repopulate the deserted lands and to establish centralized villages. In the period between 1745 and 1784, when the estates were returned to their owners or to their heirs, the SSPCK opened a large number of spinning schools. In addition to the schoolhouse and schoolroom there were farm buildings, workshops, gardens and farm land. Provision was made for apprenticeships to blacksmiths, cartwrights, shoemakers and so on. Although the movement had begun to decline after 1784, in 1795 there were still as many as 229 ordinary schools with 12,010 pupils, and 94 industrial schools with 2,360 pupils. These were in addition to the parochial schools, established since the time of James I, and a large number of private schools.

In time the spinning schools lost their special character and offered a curriculum indistinguishable from the ordinary elementary schools and, although they continued to receive a Government grant until 1832, they had by this time become merely protestant boarding schools. The function of the spinning schools had been entirely different from that of the parochial and elementary schools which had always provided an academic curriculum through which a small number of boys could receive personal advancement either in the Church or in secular employment as clerks or schoolteachers. The SSPCK schools set out to provide an education in the skills necessary to sustain a viable agricultural community. Seen as an exercise in social reconstruction through agricultural education, the SSPCK experiments which trained thousands of scholars over more than a century, were not entirely unsuccessful and had a lasting effect in stimulating Scottish agriculture and strengthening life in highland communities.

The community colleges

The most widely known of all initiatives in British rural education – the Cambridgeshire village colleges of Henry Morris – was also inspired by the desire to use the educational system to support a declining rural community. Although concerned with the social rather than the economic basis of the community, the village college movement in many ways echoes the theme of the SSPCK's endeavours. As head of the Cambridgeshire education service from 1924 to 1953 Morris singlemindedly pursued a personal vision. He is quoted by Ree (1973): 'The task of education is to convert society into a series of cultural communities . . . where every local community should become an education society, and education would not merely be the consequence of education.'

During the 1920s Morris observed the decline of the traditional power of the landowning class and the resulting lack of community leadership. It was his hope, and to some extent also his fear, that this leadership would be grasped by the ordinary people themselves. He saw the village colleges as the symbolic and actual centre of this new leadership: 'Without some such institution as the village college a rural community consisting largely of agricultural workers, small proprietors and small farmers will not be equal to the task of maintaining a worthy rural civilisation.' There are tones of pessimism as well as elitism in this sentence for it is precisely this class which has maintained a distinctive culture in rural Wales for two hundred years. High land prices from 1914 to 1925 led a sizeable proportion of the landed class to sell out and reinvest in more profitable sectors of the economy. With the onset of the depression years the countryside suffered not only from financial hardship but from a demoralization caused by the withdrawal of its traditional leadership. Morris submitted his plan to Cambridgeshire Education Committee in 1924. He proposed ten village colleges to provide for:

> . . . the co-ordination and development of all forms of education: primary, secondary, further and adult education, including agricultural education, together with social and recreational facilities and at the same time furnish a community centre for the neighbourhood . . . the narrower conception associated with the isolated elementary school would be abolished. (Ree, 1973)

Neither the education committee nor the Ministry of Education (nor indeed the local people themselves) were willing to provide all the funds for the village colleges and Morris personally raised large contributions from charitable trusts in America as well as in Britain. The first college was opened at Sawston in 1930 by the Prince of Wales. It contained a library, open in the evenings, and a number of community facilities. In 1937 the second college at Bottisham and Linton was opened, and two years later the best known of all the village colleges, which Morris had managed to have designed by Gropius and Fry, was opened at Impington. The last opened in 1967, making a total of twelve village colleges in Cambridgeshire. They were an extraordinary achievement and were recognized as such at the time. They provided a secondary education for a large number of rural children at a time when the idea that secondary education should be provided for non-academic children was by no means accepted.

The colleges now cater for pupils between the ages of eleven and sixteen. In Cambridgeshire sixth-form education is centred on a small number of large schools and further education establishments. The importance of the village colleges as a community resource is still recognized. As an example, Sawsey, one of the smaller colleges, serving an area with eleven villages and a total population of 8,000, has 510 full-time pupils and 32 teachers including some part-time staff. As many as 768 adults are enrolled for formal classes, 782 attend in self-functioning associations, 265 young people are members of the youth centre and many others use its outdoor facilities. In addition, the college is involved in various community service projects and is booked each weekend for dances, parties, receptions and so on. Its own transport system is in use day and night.

Defenders of the village college concept argue that it is essential to maintain the disparate functions of the college – school, community centre, further education provision, clinic, careers advisory office, library and so on – under the control of a single authority. Only in this way can the necessary inspiration be maintained. The appointment of a headteacher/warden is thus more than a symbolic gesture but indicates the continued commitment of the local education authority to the idea of the village colleges.

Not all village colleges have been successful. Some have been ignored by outlying villages (which had lost their own school), but in other cases the failure was due to an unsympathetic headteacher. The success or failure of the colleges seems to depend upon the ability and willingness of the headteacher/warden. A village college without a positive commitment to community education and without a distinguishing curriculum (a development which Morris had resisted) becomes an unremarkable secondary modern school and that is just what happened to some of them during the 1950s.

This has been noted by many critics who find the system of control by headteacher/warden a source of weakness rather than strength. Butler and Morgan (1966) feel that, although education is a continuous process, compulsory full-time education and voluntary part-time education are so different in kind that only an exceptional individual can be the ultimate authority in both spheres at the same time. The argue that a headteacher must be instinctively authoritarian, that the organizer of adult education must be instinctively democratic, and that the two attitudes can co-exist but only uneasily in one man. They further perceive the headteacher/warden as a threat to the independent development of a professionally run adult education service and regard the adult education tutor as more important than his subordinate position to the headteacher/warden allows. Cambridgeshire and a number of others LEAs influenced by the village college concept see the role of headteacher/warden as essential to ensure community education and, administratively, as the only way of preventing damaging tensions between the adult education function and the secondary education function. Butler and Morgan reject the first argument as not worth serious consideration: no one supposes that one man should have authority over both primary and secondary education on the grounds that education is a continuous process so why should it be necessary to impose a single authority over secondary and adult education? They further reject the idea that disputes would inevitably break out over the use of joint facilities. They suggest that adult education should be removed from the village colleges and placed under the authority of an area institute of further education which would embrace a number of school sites. Such an organization would be superior to the village college system and could be staffed by full-time professional tutors. Adult education would thus be better able to develop its own career structure independently of the secondary school teachers. The headteacher/warden, they point out, is always appointed first as a headteacher.

This professional squabble accounts for at least some of the failure of the village colleges to spread far beyond their original county. In fact, the concept of community education, despite the success of the Cambridgeshire scheme, later proved to be more fruitful in urban areas and, though there are a number of village colleges in Cumberland, Derbyshire and a few other English counties, the best known of the modern community schools are now those in Manchester, Coventry and in predominantly urban areas of Leicestershire.

The selective function of rural education

We have noted that the SSPCK schools had as their purpose the strengthening of rural society through education in agricultural skills, but education in rural Britain, and most particularly in Scotland, has generally fulfilled an entirely different function. Synge (1975) has made a valuable contribution to our understanding of this process. He observes that the rapidly developing Scottish economy of the eighteenth and nineteenth centuries stimulated the growth of Scottish education and, since the English educational system was underdeveloped, England offered attractive opportunities for educated Scots. The nonconformist character of Wales and Scotland has long been associated with a high level of educational provision and, although the reasons are complex, it is worth noting that the noncomformist churches stressed the need for individuals to read the Scriptures and to reach a personal understanding of the Word of God. This was clearly the case in eighteenth-century Wales where a network of circulating schools, organized by the Reverend Griffith Jones and staffed by peripatetic teachers, taught many thousands of children and adults to read the Welsh Bible. It has been claimed that these schools, which met in chapels and farmhouses, made Wales the first literate nation in Europe. Synge shows that the educational system of rural England was characterized even more than that of urban England by class segregation. Provision of schools was generally less extensive in the rural areas than the towns. There was considerable opposition by school officers to the introduction of anything but the most elementary subjects and the rural working class had little interest in education. At secondary level the academic grammar schools, particularly in the rural areas, were almost exclusively for the middle class and, where they did admit working-class pupils, the standards are reported to have been low. Those who controlled the system, churchmen in particular, saw no reasons to change it.

In Scotland, the Church took an entirely different position and encouraged the idea that schools should be supported by people of all classes – even as late as the mid-nineteenth century some landowners sent their children to the local parish school. Synge argues that the lack of any distinction between elementary and academic secondary education (which was strictly enforced in England) meant that an academic education was open to the rural middle class and to some lower-class pupils. In 1830 nearly half of the parishes had at least one teacher who had spent four years at university – a situation that was certainly not true at that time (or probably at any time since) in England. The difference between Scottish and English attitudes towards education can be seen in the pattern of charitable support. Private charities and bequests in Scotland supported training college and university scholarships for able scholars from rural schools while in England charities tended to favour the establishment of rural craft centres rather than scholarships. Synge shows that these differences in the provision of education were real in their effects. Of the intellectual elite of eighteenth-century Britain, 20 per cent of eminent Scots were from farming families compared with only 6 per cent of eminent Englishmen. At that time access to university was much greater in rural Scotland than in England. Between 1730 and 1839, 17 per cent of the matriculated students of Glasgow University were the sons of landless tenant farmers whereas at Cambridge, over the same period, none of the graduates were from that class.

In Wales the same pattern developed, if belatedly. The case of Wales is particularly interesting. When the University Colleges were founded in the 1880s the secondary school system was quite inadequate and unable to provide a sufficient number of well prepared students. Following the Aberdare enquiry the 1889 Intermediate Education Act was passed enabling locally elected school bodies to establish new county schools. These were often based on older grammar schools but several new schools were created.

In the nineteenth century the land in Wales was owned by an anglicized and Anglican aristo-gentry class which had little in common with its Welsh-speaking nonconformist tenantry. The history of nineteenth-century Wales is the history of the struggle between these classes. The power of the landowning class was almost total and, although they provided Church schools where their tenants' children could learn English and the rudiments of arithmetic, they did not provide any kind of secondary education. The struggle between these groups was determined by the extension of the franchise. In 1887, when the county councils were formed, the landowning class suffered what was to prove a permanent political defeat as the tenant farmers elected their own candidates and rejected the landowners.

When the control of education passed to the county councils, with the creation of the LEAs in 1902, the councillors undertook to increase steadily the number of grammar school places precisely in order to provide for those children who could not expect to remain in farming. In England, where there were no differences of language or religion between the landowners and the tenants, the landowning class was able to survive the introduction of democratic local elections and saw no reason to provide more than a minimum number of secondary school places.

The extensive grammar school provision in Wales is a matter of record. The Robbins Report (1963) showed clearly that the Welsh rural counties provided grammar school places for up to a third of their secondary school pupils and this pattern has persisted under comprehensive reorganization. Byrne *et al.* (1975) show that six Welsh rural counties were distinctive for their high level of educational provision. In 1970 in these LEAs, 41.3 per cent of pupils remained at school until the age of 16 compared with 31.2 per cent in most English rural LEAs; 8.3 per cent were awarded university grants compared with 7.2 per cent; 13.2 per cent were awarded full time further education awards compared with 6.9 per cent; 6.7 per cent were awarded lesser awards for further education compared with 2.8 per cent; 8.9 per cent were awarded teacher training awards compared with 6 per cent. And all this despite the fact that these were relatively poor counties compared with many English rural counties.

It can be argued that the explanation for this remarkable pattern, which is unclear to Byrne *et al.*, is to be found in the determination of the Welsh farming community to exploit the opportunities offered by education for social and geographical mobility. That the effects of such differences in the perceived function of education should persist within the comprehensive schools is testimony to the power of the patterns created in the early decades of this century.

A rural curriculum

The SSPCK schools and the village colleges, although both intended to support the local community, had one notable difference. The village colleges did not attempt to provide a locally relevant curriculum. Rural studies has two quite distinct meanings: education for rural children and education about the natural environment. It was the first aspect which led to its historical appearance on the school curriculum.

Rolls (1965) divides developments in rural education (rural studies in my usage) in this century into three periods: the first from about 1900 to the mid-1930s, the second from then until about 1950 and the third from 1950 and 1965. During the first period when the purpose of rural education was understood as being to prepare pupils for life in the countryside, the schools aimed to provide courses directly relevant to employment in agriculture and horticulture. At this time, courses in gardening and livestock keeping were introduced into many rural schools. Between 1930 and 1950 the emphasis changed. The Board of Education pamphlet (1934) *Education and the Countryside* was at pains to stress that it was not primarily concerned with the vocational training of those who would would earn their livelihood in the country districts but with the various ways in which schools could make the study of the natural environment contribute to a good general education. To a large extent this change of policy recognized the declining importance of the traditional skills of husbandry as farming became increasingly affected by advances in agricultural science and technology. Moreover, increasing mechanization had reduced the demand for farm labour and it was apparent that substantial numbers of country children would have to find work outside agriculture and, in all probability, in the towns and cities. The schools responded by introducing courses in rural science and left vocational training to the colleges of agriculture and farm institutes which were introduced at this time. Since 1950 this policy has continued and the emphasis is now firmly on the need to provide a general education for rural children, especially on exploring the uses teachers can make of the natural environment. This is made clear in the Ministry of Education (1958) pamphlet *Schools and the Countryside* which set out to explore '. . . the educational opportunities offered by the countryside to all schools whether they be rural schools or urban schools'. The mention of urban schools, in the context of this discussion, marked a new shift of emphasis.

There are two broadly distinct modes of introducing rural studies into the curriculum. The first is to introduce a rural bias into the teaching of suitable subjects, for example, history, science, mathematics and so on; the second is to introduce specially designed courses in rural science, for example, rural biology or environmental studies, which can be offered for examination at Certificate of Secondary Education and General Certificate of Education level. Despite some remarkable experiments with integrated studies, the latter approach has been most widely adopted. The growth of rural studies in this latter model has been steady with the National Rural Studies Association acting as a focus for development.

However, the integrated studies model gave rise to some of the most fascinating experiments in rural studies and the reasons for their failure are sociologically interesting. The introduction of universal secondary education after 1944 stimulated interest in rural studies in several English counties. Hilton and Audric (1946), for example, give a detailed account of Lingfield County Secondary School which offered a wide variety of courses based on agriculture and horticulture. It was in Wales, however, that the best known innovations were made.

It has already been shown that in Scotland and Wales the educational system has had an obvious selective function and that the academic curriculum of the grammar school was kept uncontaminated by rural studies. The exclusively academic nature of the Welsh secondary school curriculum was not maintained without a struggle. There was considerable pressure from the LEAs through the Welsh Joint Board of Education to develop courses in rural studies but, in spite of the efforts of individual inspectors, the Welsh Department of the Board of Education remained firmly opposed to the introduction of non-academic courses. It attempted in the 1930s to prevent Cardiganshire LEA from providing ten acre smallholdings for its new non-academic secondary schools. Its report, *Education in*

Rural Wales (1947), was cautious in tone and only suggested that secondary modern schools in rural areas could introduce general science with an emphasis on biology, which might be linked to practical work in farm and garden, as a good foundation for the study of agriculture. Regardless of the unfavourable stance of the central authority, the more adventurous LEAs established a number of farm schools during these years. Two of these, Clyro Court and Pembrokeshire Grammar School, are particularly interesting.

Clyro Court served a remote and sparsely populated farming area in the Wye Valley. Its thirty acre farm, managed by two full-time workmen, included an orchard and forestry plantation and was stocked with sheep, cows, pigs and poultry. The workshop, laboratory and craftsroom were fully used. The curriculum included biology (with plant and animal nutrition and growth), book-keeping, toolmaking, domestic economy (including cheese and butter making), bacon curing, milking, cookery, needlework and so on. It was able to provide a range of social activities in co-operation with the Young Farmers Club and arranged part-time classes for school leavers.

In 1955 Pembrokeshire Grammar School moved to a new site with a hundred acres of farm, woodland and gardens. Only one in seven of the pupils were from a rural background, and only one in fourteen or fifteen were from farming families. The technical course (the school took 38 per cent of the age group at this time) was mainly confined to the boys from outlying farms who were boarded in the school, but the farm was used for a variety of activities involving a large proportion of the schools' children.

These experiments were assessed by the Central Advisory Council for Education (Wales) (1960). Again the overall judgement was cool. The report noted an 'obvious risk of over-emphasis' in the Clyro Court curriculum and warned that the farm might come to dominate the whole of the curriculum 'to such an extent that a liberal education becomes impossible'. Of the Pembroke curriculum the report was sceptical of the ability of pupils to derive the principles of, for example, O–level physics from farm based studies and thought the scheme 'only visibly successful in the teaching of biology'. They felt, also, that

31

students could be prevented from studying other subjects at a theoretical level and asked why, if this was such a good way to teach biology, was the scheme restricted to the technical stream only. The report did not recommend farm studies for grammar schools despite its own regret that well qualified Welsh students were not applying in sufficient numbers for courses in the Welsh agricultural colleges, which were consequently obliged to accept students from England. It tentatively suggested that an LEA might introduce one experimental farm school of a bi-lateral or comprehensive type in a Welsh-speaking area but clearly felt that the farm school curriculum was too likely to become unbalanced and a threat to the essential elements of liberal education – art, music and literature – which were not essentially related to farm life. The cautious, if not hostile, attitude of the report did not encourage further experiments in this direction, and Clyro Court was eventually closed after barely more than twenty years and is now an hotel. The farm at the now fully comprehensive Pembroke school is still worked and is used as the foundation for its biology through agriculture course taught throughout the school to CSE and GCE O–level. The central Welsh authorities, the Welsh Department of the Board of Education and its successor, the Welsh Education Office, in particular, have shown a consistent determination to maintain the academic character of the grammar schools (and the comprehensive schools) and to confine agricultural and horticultural studies to a subordinate place on the secondary school curriculum. The effects of this policy are still apparent so that it is possible, for example, for pupils to study horticultural science to GCE A–level in England but not in Wales.

The modern conception of rural studies, as defined by the Schools Council Working Paper 24 (1969), emphasizes the change of direction in rural studies. It defines rural education as 'the study of the environment in and around the school with particular reference to animals and plants important to man and leading to an understanding of man's interaction with the countryside'. The aims of rural education should include:

1 Making the public aware of the need for the conservation of the natural resources of the countryside.

2 Environmental studies (education through the environment) involving a complex of subjects of which rural studies might well prove most important.
3 Recognition that the educational opportunities offered by the subject are wide and have advantages as a basis for the construction of an integrated course of study at all levels.
4 An understanding that the intellectual disciplines within rural studies are considerable and are being identified.

But the ghosts of former days still haunt the garden plots of many a comprehensive school. Only a minority of rural children were ever taught in schools like Clyro Court and for the majority 'rural studies' meant hard work in the school garden. The Schools Council report was particularly concerned to rid the subject of this unfavourable image for the evidence is that rural studies still have an important secondary function. Rolls (1965), reporting a survey of the National Rural Studies Association shows that 34 per cent of the non-academic secondary modern schools possessed a school garden, but few were found in grammar schools. It is not without significance that, in England and Wales, rural studies has been largely confined to the secondary modern schools and is now confined to the lower streams of the comprehensive schools. In one comprehensive school studied recently, horticulture is reserved for those boys who have been considered unsuitable for an academic course for reasons which have more to do with maintenance of control than with providing a course suited to their abilities. Even the CSE regulations, which allow credit to be given for practical study, mean that up to 40 per cent of the course marks can be given for practical work without disadvantage, which, if it doesn't actually encourage the old pattern, at least permits it to continue.

Ironically, it may be in urban schools that this traditional pattern has been decisively broken. The comparatively recent interest in rural studies by urban schools has led to a number of noteworthy experiments. Cadbury (1974) describes the Chapmans Hill School Farm Experiment. This seventy acre mixed farm on the outskirts of Birmingham was visited in its first year by 5,570 pupils and used as a basis for project work. The farm produces a small profit and provides a base for instruction in rural science for a large number of urban schools. Young's (1968) publication, issued by the Association of Agriculture and offering suggestions for teachers and a collection of resource material, indicates the continuing interest of official bodies in the teaching of studies relevant to agriculture in schools.

Conclusion

This chapter has attempted to draw out the underlying themes which have characterized rural education since the development of formal schooling. Throughout its history decisions have been made about the purpose of rural education, its content, and to whom it should be taught. One theme has been the attempt to use the educational system as a means of supporting or reconstructing the economic and social structure of the countryside. The SSPCK spinning schools and the Cambridgeshire village colleges were both intended to fulfil this function although in obviously different ways. The spinning schools were designed to strengthen the economic structure through vocational training; the village colleges were intended to be the centre of a liberal culture and their curriculum was indistinguishable from any other non-academic secondary school. But there is an important sense in which they shared the same aims.

A second theme has been the selective function of the rural secondary schools. In Scotland and in Wales, especially, the function of the academic secondary schools was understood as being to provide scholars with qualifications which offered opportunities for social (and geographical) mobility; the introduction of courses in agriculture, which would have sent them straight back to the poor farms they came from, was seen as obviously self-defeating. The determined resistance of the central authorities to courses leading to agricultural work (despite the lack of home candidates for the Welsh colleges of agriculture) is well documented and demonstrates that this was no accidental consequence of the 'Welsh concern with education' but the result of a considered policy which is still influential in its effects.

The attempts to introduce locally relevant knowledge – rural studies – into the secondary schools has generally to be seèn as a

34

failure. Agricultural work had such a low status that the grammar schools never contemplated the introduction of courses with a rural bias. In the new non-academic secondary schools some of the most interesting innovations met with official disfavour and were gradually dropped as the changing rural economy made traditional courses in domestic farm crafts irrelevant and as the new county colleges took responsibility for agricultural training. Not until the 1960s did new examination courses in agricultural biology and horticulture become accepted as an ordinary part of the comprehensive school curriculum. Even now these courses are regarded in many schools as the preserve of the lower ability sets. Time will show whether the recent concern with the natural environment, which has led to some interesting experiments in city schools, will re-establish rural studies as worthwhile for all children.

3

Differences and disadvantages

Research concerned with differences in the intellectual abilities of urban and rural children has a long history. Most of the work has its origins in the traditions of American rural sociology and mental testing and has generally shown that urban children perform better on standardized tests of attainment than rural children. In fact, there is a remarkable dearth of reliable research data. Barr (1959), in what is still the most recent comprehensive review, observes that it is often alleged that children from rural areas are intellectually and educationally inferior to their urban contemporaries. He notes that this is variously explained by the inferior intelligence of the rural population, or the out-migration of abler families to the town, or the unstimulating environment, or the poorer quality of the schools. None of these explanations (which in any case beg the facts) can be supported without considerable qualification.

The most extensive studies of the distribution of intelligence in the population are the Scottish Mental Surveys of 1932, 1947 and 1954. Barr's article shows that the 1932 Scottish Mental Survey found no real differences between the abilities of children in the rural and urban regions of Scotland and, although the succeeding survey in 1947 did find a very small but statistically significant difference in verbal IQ test scores in favour of urban children, this difference was less than the average difference between boys and girls in Scotland and indicates little.

The out-migration hypothesis seems to have a little more support but the evidence is confusing. The 1947 survey found that the average score of city-born children (in the national sample) moving to the countryside was 36.1, whereas the average score of those who moved from the countryside to the town was 43.2. While it is possible to understand the high scores of out-migrants from the countryside there seems to be no good explanation for the low scores of those migrating to the countryside. The following 1954 survey enabled an analysis to be made of children with extreme high and extreme low scores. It was found that most of the high scores came from the cities, 46.5 per cent, and that most of the low scores came from the rural areas, 29.7 per cent. Conversely, 55.7 per cent of low scores were found in the rural areas compared with 21 per cent in the cities. The problem here is to allow for the known social class differences associated both with the distribution of IQ scores and with the pattern of occupations in the towns and the countryside.

Rural sociology, as I pointed out in chapter 1, has given support to the idea that the rural environment is lacking in challenge and intellectual stimulation. So it is hardly surprising that this has been seen as an explanation of the relatively poor performance of rural children in the 11+ examination which has been found in several studies. Barr reports that studies of 11+ results in Cambridgeshire, Wiltshire and Kent revealed a noticeable superiority of urban over rural children, and it is known that in the 1950s and 1960s some English rural counties made additional grammar school places available to children from small rural schools which were not gaining the statistically expected proportion of 11+ successes. The National Foundation for Educational Research (1961) in its National Survey also found that the highest proportion of able pupils was concentrated in the urban areas as was reflected in the proportion of pupils gaining grammar school places. For example, in

Cambridgeshire over a ten year period, 24 per cent of urban candidates in the 11+ examination gained grammar school places compared with only 20 per cent of rural candidates. There is evidence to suggest that part of this difference was due to the practice of middle-class parents living in the country removing their children from village schools to better equipped schools in the towns. Barr is able to show, incidentally, that these generally poor results were not an artefact of the testing situation nor the result of inherent bias in the tests themselves.

The problem with all of these studies, as Barr points out, is that social class is not taken into account. Where it has been, as in Douglas (1968), the crude urban–rural differences in attainment and intelligence scores disappear. Although it is still generally true that a greater proportion of middle-class occupations are found in the urban areas, it is important to remember that the social class composition of urban areas does, of course, vary and, just as cities are not socially homogeneous, neither is the countryside. The social composition of a Hertfordshire commuter village is very different from that of a Northumberland estate village. Indeed, the search for urban–rural differences is probably misconceived and Pahl's (1966) stricture is worth repeating: 'Any attempt to tie particular patterns of social relationships to specific geographical millieux is a singularly fruitless exercise.' The evidence for urban–rural differences is, therefore, hard to find. Moreover, properly interpreted, what little evidence there is suggests quite the opposite. It has already been shown in chapter 2 that the highest educational attainments are made by a handful of poor rural counties; to suppose that they achieve this despite a naturally lesser intelligent stock is simply perverse. The evidence for the selective migration hypothesis is also unconvincing. It should be remembered that the 1947 Scottish survey was carried out at a time of particular economic difficulty, and it is not known whether the same general pattern would be found in future studies.

Deprivation and disadvantage

To begin with many writers use the words interchangeably. Deprivation is considered the stronger and, although it is now out of favour, as Rutter and Madge's (1976) discussion illustrates, it remains intimately linked with the concepts of cultural and linguistic deprivation. The former has been adequately criticized in this series by Robinson (1976) and the latter by Stubbs (1976). Let it be noted here that, as those writers point out, these concepts derive from a view of culture and language which is not sociologically informed. To say (as the Plowden Report does) that gypsies are culturally deprived is to deny the reality of the obviously distinctive culture that gypsies value; to say (as Schools Council Working Paper 27 (1970) does) that working-class children are linguistically deprived is to deny that social class dialects are able to conceptualize children's experiences, and there has been sufficient work in sociology and socio-linguistics to show that this is not the case. The ethnographic studies of native American schooling by Wax and Wax (1964) and Dumont and Wax (1976) are well known examples.

Sociologists, for example Runciman (1966), have found the concept of relative deprivation useful for it draws attention to certain obvious fallacies. It is not sensible to say, to take a daft example, that Henry VIII was deprived because he couldn't watch Starsky and Hutch. Deprivation is only meaningful if it is experienced as such in a socially relevant context. So I do not regard myself as deprived because I can't afford to eat at the Savoy Grill, but I certainly would if I couldn't afford a fish supper like everyone else in my neighbourhood. Sharp (1974) argues that a non-normative definition of deprivation must involve recognition of an individual's own subjective realization of his deprivation. An individual must know that he lacks something which he both wants and is prevented from having. A normative definition involves not only a judgement that he is deprived of something but a moral judgement that he should be provided with it. There are, however, nagging problems with this relativist position; in a degenerate form it can easily become an excuse for doing nothing to alleviate poverty both at home and abroad, but the problems associated with the normative position seem even greater.

Disadvantage can be used in a generally weaker sense and is most typically used to describe material and attitudinal factors which can hinder educational progress. A child who lives in a home where the income is £6,000 a year is materially advantaged in comparison with a child living in a home where the income is £30 a week supplementary benefit, and a child who attends a well equipped adequately staffed school has more advantages than a child attending a poorly equipped and under staffed school.

The dominant theory of educational disadvantage arose as an explanation of the poor educational attainments of children in the inner city areas. The theory is American in origin but has been readily accepted in Britain. The Plowden Report (1967), influenced by surveys which showed the extent of material deprivation (i.e. poverty) in the inner cities, proposed that these districts should be designated as Educational Priority Areas. The committee felt that the needs of these areas could best be met by good sound primary schools and recommended that teachers working in those areas should receive a higher income (in order to retain them in poor areas at a time of teacher shortage) and that the older schools should be replaced or remodelled as soon as practicable. The first EPA grants went entirely to the urban areas but it was soon found that on the criterion used – the percentage of pupils receiving free school meals – some schools in rural areas had as many disadvantaged pupils as some of those in the inner cities. On this basis rural Gwynedd once calculated that it had a greater proportion of such pupils than Liverpool.

The knowledge that there are children of poor families living in the countryside really ought not to have come as a surprise. But it has given rise to a new concern with what has already been called rural disadvantage. If I object to this term it is because it perpetuates the Plowden fallacy of confounding two distinct levels of analysis, that of disadvantaged children and that of disadvantaged areas. If some rural children live in poverty, and if their material conditions are responsible for their poor performance in the educational system (which has to be shown), then that is not a disadvantage caused by the conditions of rural living but one caused by poverty and is an economic, not a rural, disadvantage. To call it such is an unnecessary mystification.

In chapter 1 it was stated that there were perhaps only two differences between urban and rural life in Britain: the low population density and the smaller local market in the countryside. Both are sometimes regarded as being disadvantages in themselves. It is worth discussing this view in some detail.

Geographical isolation

There is a view that isolation is in itself a form of deprivation or disadvantage. Children who live on remote farms are held to be disadvantaged because they are cut off from contact with others. Those who hold this view usually know little of the social world of farming families and confuse geographical or spatial isolation with social isolation. Geographical isolation is rarely a factor which can in itself be identified as having necessary sociological consequences. It is evident that apparently similar isolated communities have been differentially influenced by cultural movements originating in more centrally placed communities. For example, the Gaelic languages have survived most strongly in Scotland, on Harris, and in Ireland, on the Arran islands. But Manx Gaelic did not survive on the Isle of Man and, in Shetland, the old Scandinavian language still spoken in the Faeroes, has gone, although Shetland is by far the most remote part of Britain. Geographical isolation is not in itself enough to prevent cultural interaction and change.

Just as geographical isolation is no necessary barrier to cultural contact and social change, neither is the city, with its vast possibilities for such interactions, a necessary obstacle to social and cultural isolation. The ghetto is an island within a city. Indeed, ghetto actually meant a physically enclosed area of a city, but the divided cities of Londonderry and Belfast are sufficient evidence that an actual barrier is not essential. In these cities effective ghettos have developed where the possibilities of social interaction with other groups can be minimized, and indeed, as Boal (1974) shows for Belfast, precisely in order to minimize such interactions. Where a geographically isolated area also becomes an effective ghetto, then the effects of both may combine to create a society which is strongly resistant to outside influence. Extremes of isolation, such as that experienced by the Tasmanians, whose island was cut off from all contact with the Australian mainland in pre-historic times, does

41

seem to produce cultural degeneration. Archaeologists can show that the number and quality of their artefacts declined over the millenia, but even then they survived until exterminated by European settlers.

The point of this is to illustrate that to speak of rural children living on a small village estate or on a hill farm as isolated, and therefore deprived of cultural contact, is to totally misunderstand the extent of isolation necessary to produce such effects on a community.

Market size

The urban concentration of services – banks, schools, shops, theatres, hotels, museums, cinemas, libraries, factories, hospitals, workshops, markets, county offices and so on and so forth – makes obvious economic sense. It necessarily implies that certain services are thus removed from the rural setting and are not easily available to the people living there. In my own case it is a handicap of sorts that, although I have plenty of space to fly them, the nearest model aeroplane shop is fifty miles away in Liverpool. There is not a large enough market in North Wales for such a shopkeeper to make a living. As a more serious example, anyone in need of urgent or regular medical attention of a specialist kind has to make long and expensive journeys to a centrally located hospital. The bigger the town or city, the greater the market and the greater the range of potential (although perhaps not actual) choice in respect of job opportunities, entertainment, consumer goods, and even marriage partners.

There is an important sense, too, in which the dominance of the centre can reduce the possibility of economic development in the periphery and may actually depend upon the underdevelopment of the periphery as a source of available labour in times of expansion, which can be left unregarded in times of recession. In this sense it is possible to argue that the rural areas are disadvantaged, and it is a disadvantage that will be experienced by, for example, a child who must spend an hour or more a day on a bus journey to school, or a school leaver who is forced to leave the area for lack of local employment opportunities.

This will be discussed more fully in chapter 9.

But it seems essential to distinguish between the necessary conditions of rural living, which have to be accepted as objective circumstances, and those which result from the withdrawal of once taken-for-granted services or from the denial, on narrow economic grounds, of socially desired goods. It seems mistaken, for example, to regard rural children as disadvantaged merely because they lack ready access to art galleries, theatres, fourteen-form-entry comprehensive schools and all the other facilities of the city; and equally mistaken to regard urban children as disadvantaged by their lack of immediate access to the sea and the woods and the mountains, to wild life and social evenings at the Young Farmers Club. There is an unmistakable tendency to discuss such locational differences as disadvantages and it is one that should be resisted.

Educational disadvantage in rural areas

Knox (1975), in a study of social malaise in different areas of England and Wales, listed fifty-three variables which might be taken as indicative of social well-being or its opposite. These included rateable values, bronchial deaths, GP case loads, the number of adults who left school before the age of fifteen, car ownership, provision of libraries, divorce rates, welfare accommodation, population migration and so on. The four most significant variables, which seemed to diagnose most comprehensively the differences between the various regions of England and Wales, were identified as:

1 Average number of persons per room.
2 Percentage of households without baths.
3 Percentage of economically active persons.
4 Percentage of persons aged sixty and over.

On these criteria the least disadvantaged county was Buckinghamshire and the most disadvantaged area was Gateshead. The most advantaged areas were those rural and semi-rural areas of rich agricultural land and prosperous commuter villages and suburbs. The least advantaged were the northern industrial towns (Wigan, St Helens, South Shields and so on), and Cumberland, Cornwall and some of the remote counties of western Wales. In these predominantly rural areas the reasons can be attributed to the poor returns from marginal agriculture, low wages, the in-migration of retired persons coupled with the out-migration of economically active younger persons, and the problems associated with seasonal employment in the holiday trade.

This problem was encountered earlier. In the northern industrial towns and in the poorer English counties, these indices of material poverty (which apart from the matter of the age structure of the population is what they are) are indeed associated with low educational attainment. That they cannot be regarded as a sufficient cause of low attainment is demonstrated by the high educational performance of the Welsh rural counties. In fact, the same pressures from the centre, which led to low educational provision in the English counties, produced in Wales a quite different mode of adaptation. In Wales, because of the circumstances discussed in chapter 2, the schools were used to provide a route out of the very conditions which, in other rural areas, were used to excuse the necessity to provide more than a minimum level of educational provision.

It has already been argued that farming people and others living in remote areas are not disadvantaged by the isolation they experience; however, this is not the conventional view, and two recent studies have attempted to examine the extent of so-called rural disadvantage in parts of Britain.

Owen (1977) locates the reasons for rural disadvantage essentially in the material conditions of life:

> Families without cars are obviously in greatest danger of cultural and geographical isolation, although mothers and pre-school children in one-car families can be house-bound and hamlet-bound for the greater part of every weekday. Total immersion in a monotonous daily routine of house and/or farm activity without any counteracting life-enhancing experience can have a devastating effect on mental health and many young mothers complain of depression, stagnation and overwork (often synonymous with boredom). In recent years the closure of rail services in rural areas has

restricted still further the movement of no-car and one-car families. Bus services are usually inadequate and are, in many cases, limited to one market bus a week.

There is not much evidence to support Owen's opinions about the effects of doing housework in an isolated dwelling. It should be easy enough to locate the proportion of rural and urban housewives prescribed anti-depressants and until that is done I would regard the notion as unproven. In what seems the most relevant study, Rutter *et al.* (1975) have found that the incidence of psychological disturbance is much higher in urban London than in the predominantly rural Isle of Wight. What we should understand is that, in recent decades, the villages have lost many of their self-sufficient functions. They have lost shops, schools (at least 129 have closed in Devon since the end of the war) and so on, thus increasing their dependence on the towns while, at the same time, public transport has been reduced or terminated altogether. Thus, people who cannot afford a car are cut off from services to which they formerly had access.

It must be stressed that the connection between material disadvantage and educational disadvantage is still unclear. Owen reports that teachers who receive children from some remote areas of Devon are in firm agreement about the effects of those conditions on adjustment to school life and subsequent progress. According to the teachers the children suffer from nine identifiable handicaps. Most of these concern the children's lack of confidence in the unfamiliar setting of an infants reception class, but two points are particularly interesting. Teachers claim that the children lack the ability to receive instructions and information because of, on the one hand, different attitudes, accents, linguistic structures and vocabulary, and on the other, restricted horizons and lack of independence. The first is the linguistic deprivation hypothesis in its usual teacher form; there is, in fact, no known Devon dialect significantly different in its linguistic structure from standard English. The second notion, that rural children's horizons are limited, presumably has some meaning to those who hold it but, without an adequate elaboration of its context, little can be said. Usually, teachers who talk like this mean that the children have never been further than the nearest market town and that this makes them more difficult to teach than those with wider spatial experiences. Once again there is no evidence that this is anything more than the reporting of prejudice. It might be worth adding (since there is no other evidence) that, in several years of research work in rural North Wales, I have never heard a teacher make this complaint of her pupils, although the pre-school spatial experiences of children in the remote valleys of that country cannot be greater than those of children in Devon, Cornwall or Cumbria. If there is a real difference in the children's behaviour in school, then it is more likely to be caused by teachers' expectations or cultural, sub-cultural or social class differences than by their local upbringing.

It is possible that Owen himself is aware of this for he points out that rural living has considerable advantages for children, including the security of growing up in a small but relatively stable world and in close contact with adults (it does not sound patronizing in context) of considerable practical ability and resourcefulness. He further warns that the dangers of confusing differences in life style with defect are as pertinent to the rural teacher as the urban teacher.

What is, so far, the only British research into rural deprivation, has been carried out in a bilingual area of South Wales. Lloyd (1978) constructed an index of social disadvantage which is worth considering in some detail. The index, reproduced here in a slightly abridged form, consisted of three scales, and the criterion of disadvantage used was one or more adverse ratings in each of three scales, *or* two or more adverse ratings in two scales, *or* three or more adverse ratings in one scale. The several ratings are made variously by the headteacher or the classroom teacher.

Social disadvantage index

Scale A (section I)

1 Is the home isolated, thus reducing social contact with other children and adults?
2 Is the distance between home and school more than one mile?

3 Is the travelling time on the school bus more than 20 minutes?

Scale A (section II)

1 Does the child, or a sibling, receive free school meals because of financial hardship?
2 Does the child have three or more siblings living at home?
3 Is the family, to your knowledge, a family with problems or difficulties?

Scale B

1 Level of co-operation with school.
2 Did the family approach the school before registration day?
3 Child's attitude to school.
4 Child's experiential background and 'readiness' for learning.

Scale C

1 Child shows sign of fatigue.
2 Child is frequently late for school.
3 Child is frequently absent from school.
4 Child shows signs of lack of alertness in class.
5 Child's personal hygiene is unsatisfactory.
6 State of child's outer clothing is unsatisfactory.
7 State of child's underwear is unsatisfactory.
8 Adequacy of child's clothing, for example, shoes, socks, warmth and suitability of clothing in warm, cold or wet weather.

This is a fine example of the sort of panic that overcomes some researchers in their search for objectivity. The criteria of disadvantage are so tightly drawn that my own children, and those of most of my neighbours, are disadvantaged according to this index. For example, a child living on an isolated farm, more than a mile from the school and travelling for more than 20 minutes on the school bus is disadvantaged. Again, a child with two brothers and a baby sister, whose mother didn't approach the school before registration day, and who arrived late (and the school taxis are often late) is disadvantaged. There are any number of permutations. The list produced in this way was submitted to the teachers who then deleted those children who were not, *in their view*, disadvantaged in any real sense. Thus an index, which started life with all the appearance of an objective research instrument, proves at the end to be no more than a measure of teachers' attitudes. This fact is adequately demonstrated by the finding that when the analysis was completed the only significant variables (excepting that of free meals – the one index of material poverty) were those assessed by the teachers. The spatial isolation of the home, the distance between the home and the school, travelling time on the bus – all were unrelated to the analysis of disadvantage.

The children were from schools in which Welsh was the natural medium of expression in a rural and semi-rural area of South Wales. They were Welsh-speaking – and preferred to use Welsh outside school – and were about five years old. The sample consisted of two groups (thirty-two pairs matched for non-verbal IQ, linguistic background, school, teacher, date of entry into school and age), one of which was 'disadvantaged' and the other a 'control'. All but two pairs were from rural or semi-rural areas, but the smallest schools (and therefore perhaps the most isolated children) were omitted where they did not contain enough pupils to match. Lloyd, with what we must hope is not a note of disappointment, writes: 'In fact it proved surprisingly difficult to obtain two groups widely differing on criteria of deprivation, because of the general interest of the parents in the areas concerned in the well-being of their children.' She is surprised, of course, because the teachers led her to believe otherwise. The most telling relationship is that between 'disadvantage' and social class which is best presented in the form of a table (page 49).

It is hard to be convinced that this index is not merely picking up some well known teacher attitudes: children of middle-class parents are not deprived (except in the most deviant case) whereas many working-class children are. It is interesting to wonder what the findings would have been had Lloyd matched the children for social class. Although, in view of the difficulty she experienced in obtaining the sample in the first place, it is

Experimental and control groups by social class

Social class	Control group	'Disadvantaged' group
Non-manual	14	1
Manual	18	31

possible that the research might never have started. Analysis of the children's speech showed that there were no specific areas of language deficiency. Both groups showed the same general weaknesses, and observed differences in speech between the groups were ones of degree. The standard of speech, in fact, generally reflected the locality in which the children lived. It is interesting to note that, although the children were matched for non-verbal IQ at the beginning of the experiment, after two years schooling a difference had developed which was not due to statistical regression. The control group had a wider vocabulary and a better level of comprehension even after allowing for these newly developed IQ differences. The 'disadvantaged' group were inferior in language development, but there were no gross deficiencies in specific areas. By the age of 7.5 the standardized reading scores were:

Experimental and control groups by English and Welsh reading scores

Reading scores	Control group	'Disadvantaged' group
English	102	95
Welsh	97	91

So it is established that clear differences in the attainments of children initially of equal measured intelligence have developed after two years of schooling, and that these differences are associated with 'disadvantage' at home and with a relatively retarded level of language development. It is crucial to understand that the causal mechanisms of this process are wholly unexplained. The 'disadvantaged' group is actually a group of working-class children chosen by their teachers according to certain notoriously subjective criteria, whose measured IQ fell several points after their experiences in those teachers' classrooms. It is not hard to speculate that the causal factors may lie not in the home but in the school.

It must be remembered that education is one of the major agencies by which existing social class groups, and the wealth agencies and power controlled by them, are maintained. Bourdieu and Passeron (1977) have shown us that education is an instrument in the reproduction of existing social class relationships and any talk of 'disadvantage' implying that the central responsibility for the workings of the system lie outside it and not within it, is a barrier to our understanding of this relationship. It is not an accident that professional workers have a different view of education to many working-class people. To the professional worker, education is vital to the maintenance of his children's status, but to some working-class people it is of little or no importance since their objective chances of gaining access to it are negligible.

Summary and conclusion

There has been no satisfactory conclusion to the search for differences in the educational attainments of urban and rural children. The conventional view that rural children are a little slower than their urban contemporaries is hard to support on the existing evidence. Most of the surveys have found trivial differences in the abilities and attainments of rural and urban children and, even when significant differences have been found, they have disappeared when class differences have been corrected. It is, in any case, an error to oppose rural and urban as if this simple dichotomy had any necessary relationship to social differences. The differences between one rural area and another can be as great as the differences between one urban area and another as Knox's study so valuably documents. The significant distinction is not between rural and urban but between rich and poor. This point is made in an Australian context in a penetrating article by Bessant (1978). But the connection between poverty and education is by no means self-evident. It is important, in this context, to note that the poverty of the Welsh counties was one of the main reasons for the high level of educational provision in those counties.

Two notions about rural disadvantage – that the lack of an urban range of goods and services is itself a form of disadvantage and that families at the end of a farm track (although almost certainly within seven or eight miles of a market town) suffer from cultural isolation – are particularly crude but, nevertheless, often influence the decisions made by urban-based administrators. Owen's remarks quoted above and the comments of Spreadbury, a senior officer of Cambridgeshire LEA (quoted in chapter 1), happen to be published examples of the genre. Two recent attempts to identify educational disadvantage in rural areas show how, despite the extensive academic criticism of their underlying assumptions, the concepts of cultural and linguistic deprivation are being trundled out for service in the new field of rural disadvantage. Owen, for example, suggests that the material conditions of life directly affect the psychological well-being of mothers and implies that this is responsible for language deficiences and restricted horizons which, according to the teachers, characterize their children. Lloyd's work has, unfortunately, little more scientific worth than Owen's report. But it does at least demonstrate that the disadvantaged children (if her sample is assumed to be representative in this respect) are almost exclusively working-class and, we may suspect, drawn from a particular sub-cultural group. It would be worth replicating Lloyd's linguistic analysis, which suggests that gross deficiencies in language do not exist and that those which do exist – mainly in the range of vocabulary – are not ones which should produce the considerable divergence in levels of IQ and attainment which she observed. It might be more helpful if, instead of collecting from teachers more information about 'disadvantaged' children, researchers, perhaps following Newby (1977), whose study of the life styles of agricultural workers in East Anglia provide a most useful

51

model, made a start on the detailed investigation of the distinctive values of rural working-class groups. We might then find that, for these groups, the educational system is rejecting as valueless the knowledge and experiences they bring to school and thus failing to provide effective learning conditions.

4

Rural
primary schools

In the countryside the basis of the existing primary school provision was established more than a century ago at a time when children had to walk to school and when all the accommodation thought necessary was a classroom or two. Over the years, most of the old schools have been provided with basic services but, by the standards of the present day building codes, they remain inadequate. A great many have been closed and their pupils transported to larger schools either in a neighbouring village or local town.

It is obvious that a system built to provide all-age education for a large and immobile population will need adjustment to meet the needs of primary schooling for a very much smaller and more mobile population. This process of adjustment is the theme of this chapter.

Both the Plowden (1967) and Gittins (1968) reports advised that the existing provision should be reorganized. They recommended that rural education should be based on primary schools of 100 to 150 pupils, enough to provide a sufficient number of classes to allow an age range within each class of not more than two years. It was argued that neighbouring schools with fewer than 50 to 60 pupils (the minimum in Gittins' view) should be closed and the pupils transferred to newly built or substantially enlarged 'area' schools which were to be sited in prosperous villages on good lines of communication. Although it was recognized that impressive work had been done by teachers in one- and two-teacher schools, it was argued that such schools could not provide the full range of curriculum activities. The lacked both the specialist staff and the resources to provide more than a basic level of education. Moreover, the financial savings to be made by school amalgamation were substantial, and it seemed to many educationists that the area school was the obvious solution to the problem of small schools: a better product at a lower cost.

The arguments of these reports will be discussed below. It is first necessary to understand the historical context of the present situation.

The history of reorganization

School closures are not new. Under the provisions of the 1902 Education Act it was envisaged that schools with an average of below thirty pupils should be closed, and since that time the number of small schools has consistently fallen. Davies (1962), writing as Director of Education for Pembrokeshire, discusses the scale of the problem caused in that county by depopulation. In six representative schools the number on roll fell, during the period 1931–61, by an average of 65 per cent. Moreover, the decline was continuing so that schools which only thirty years ago had between fifty-eight and ninety pupils on roll, were now in danger of becoming one-teacher schools. It is not easy to obtain reliable estimates of the number of schools closed during these years, but an indication of the pace of closures during this period can be gathered from Sellman's (1968) study of school reorganization in Devonshire. The details show that the two sharpest periods of decline came during the inter-war period of agricultural depression, and immediately after the introduction of universal secondary education following the 1944 Education Act:

Primary school closures in Devon 1907–67

1907–18 8	1939–45 18	1952–60 36
1919–38 51	1946–51 68	1961–7 17

The DES' *Statistics of Education* (1961) show that even at that late date there were 1,307 schools (including thirty-three all-age schools) with fewer than twenty-five pupils on roll and 2,612 schools with between twenty-six and fifty pupils. Just fifteen years later, DES (1976) figures show that the number of schools with up to twenty-five on roll had been reduced to 320 and those with rolls between twenty-six and fifty to 1,354. The 1960s were a peak period in some areas for school closure. Transport was becoming cheaper and, as Jones (1961) indicates, LEAs were becoming increasingly conscious of the costs of keeping small schools open. His article shows that the per capita cost of small schools was many times greater than that in larger schools: a 15-pupil school cost £75 per head compared with the county average of £53. Unfortunately, there was no other analysis of the cost of school amalgamation and this averaging exercise, although of little real use, has, until recently, continued unchallenged. It should not be thought that the pace of school closures has slackened in recent years. Rogers (1977), in a study based on full replies from only twenty-seven of the forty-seven LEAs in England and Wales, revealed that since 1967, when the Plowden report recommended that the ideal size for a rural school should be between 120–60 pupils, more than 500 small schools have been closed, including 130 since county reorganization in 1975, and that a further 95 are being actively considered for closure.

The development of the local protest

There are well-defined statutory procedures which have to be followed when a school is closed. In many LEAs they became almost a matter of weekly routine. Cogan and Eyken *et al.* (1973), quote the former Chief Education Officer for Devon describing just how smoothly the routine was managed:

> Between 1950 and 1960 we closed about one hundred . . . . It isn't a negative policy; they are being closed because they're

uneconomical, educationally and financially. A small two-teacher school costs about two or three times as much per head to run as a larger school. Whatever people say, these small schools educationally can be too cosy, the quality of work not as good or as sharp as it should be. So we have a quite positive policy of setting up area schools . . . . To give one example, we closed a year or two ago in one area six schools and put them into one. Each of those schools had 30 or fewer children on roll, and we've now got a school of 180 or 200 . . . . Now how did we set about it? . . . It's a long-winded, time-taking process . . . . The CEO and his staff have to popularize, simplify and explain repeatedly and consistently in a way that civil servants are not expected to and have no need to. . . . Plans can so easily go wrong however sensible they might seem. We have a case lately where we were proposing to close one small school and send the children to a proposed new school in a village just two miles away and at the first meeting we had, there seemed to be general agreement – only 15 parents bothered to turn up – until suddenly there was an objection and an influential person in the neighbourhood got to work and another meeting was demanded. At this meeting there appeared more people than lived in the village, they all voted and they were able just to kill the idea of closing this little village school and it still remains open. I said sourly at the time that there were apparently some people who still felt that anything was good enough for country children. It may be several years before we can make a move again; probably we won't make a move until the new school is completed in the next village and the people in this village with the tiny, obsolete school realize what they are missing.

Because each closure affected only a small group of people the opposition to amalgamation plans was rarely successful. But attitudes such as those expressed above are now held less confidently and are likely to meet with swift contradiction by the middle-class organizers of save-our-village-school campaigns. Opposition to school closure is now organized on a local and regional basis and is able to attract support from national organizations. Most recently the National Consumer Council has offered financial aid to villagers who plan to maintain their school against the LEA's decision to close it. The educational magazine *Where* has monitored recent closures and offered advice to parents involved in campaigns against school amalgamation.

This change in the readiness of village communities to accept decisions from County Hall has not been properly understood. LEA officers in their more harassed moments (and angry public meetings are pretty harassing) put it down to 'agitators', but a sociologist ought to be able to say a little more. The most fundamental change has been in the attitudes of village people. In chapter 3 it was stated that a decade or two ago many middle-class children were sent by their parents to town schools known to have a high rate of success in the 11+ examination rather than to the local schools. This is no longer the practice. With the ending of 11+ selection, parents no longer see the point of sending their children out of the village and a greater awareness of the social benefits of living in a small community has made many actively opposed to the idea. Certainly, that growing section of the rural population that has chosen to live in the countryside for environmental reasons could hardly be expected not to support local institutions – and the school is one of the few left.

Secondly, the assessment of educational quality is emerging, in the popular as well as the sociological consciousness, as a political question as much as a technical question. At the moment LEA officers are still the most influential group and are usually able to impose their definitions of the situation on the key members of the Education Committee in opposition to the definitions of the villagers. But it can no longer be taken for granted by LEA officers that their judgements will be accepted. In particular, certain contradictions in the dominant educational rhetoric have been exposed. For example, the small schools which pioneered the teaching methods (family grouping, integrated studies, individual learning and so on) recommended to large schools as good practice by advisors, are yet held by those same advisors to be educationally inefficient.

Protest groups have also been effective in challenging the cost analyses made by some administrators. Hemmingford Abbots school in Cambridgeshire is a typical case. The total cost of running this two- or three-teacher school is £15,000 a year. The LEA estimated that closure of the school would result in a saving of around £10,000 but the managers, in their submission to the Education Committee, argued that transferring the children to a neighbouring school would require the use of a mobile classroom and, taking certain other factors into account, showed that the total potential savings from the planned amalgamation would be only £4,000 or 0.0007 per cent of the LEA's annual budget. It is not suggested here that the managers were right and the LEA wrong. What is significant is that LEA costings are being questioned by people who until very recently would have accepted the 'expert' view without argument.

The fact that LEAs do not agree on the minimum size of an educationally viable school adds a further complication. There is a school on one of the Scilly islands with four pupils. There are several in Wales with fewer than a dozen. It is most probable that these would be regarded as smaller than ideal, but Rogers' survey shows that policy varies from Clwyd, Wales where the policy is to retain village schools wherever possible (and it has more than twenty two-teacher schools with fewer than forty pupils each), to Nottinghamshire which regards schools with less than eighty pupils as non-viable. Since these policies are said to be held on educational grounds it would be interesting to know whether these LEAs are using different criteria of educational efficiency or sharing the criteria but disagreeing about their interpretation. In either case the disagreement exposes the non-objective character of their judgements

The importance to the community of the school has been stressed by every report on village schools: Gittins, Plowden, Schools Council and so on. But it doesn't count for much when the decisions have to be made. In fact, little is known of the real value of the school to the community. As a meeting place for adult classes and so on, its contribution to the village may seem unimportant: nothing that could not be achieved equally well by a good village hall. But it is mistaken to assess the community value of a village school in this way. The school is one of the main instruments for the transmission of knowledge and, as we know from the Welsh-medium schools in Wales, an important instrument in the transmission of local culture. A village regards its school as a sign of its continued survival as a community in itself. Research into the community use of village schools, such as that being carried out at Aston University, needs to take these sociological considerations into account.

The availability of nursery education can also be seriously threatened by closures. Garvey (1976) points out that it is the five- (and she might have added the under fives) to eight-year-olds who are least adapted for travelling and most in need of the security and the neighbourliness of village school education – qualities so firmly recommended by the Plowden Report. The small village school is usually the only nursery and playgroup available in the country areas. Garvey quotes the headteacher of an East Anglian Fen school commenting on the fate of his nursery class if the school were to close:

> The under fives would have to stay at home. It's hard enough for mothers to get about in this area as it is. They simply wouldn't take on the responsibility of trailing six miles if it wasn't compulsory. As far as nursery education in the Fen is concerned, small schools shutting would be a tragedy.

A survey of resources

There is very little research available on the material conditions of small rural schools. A Schools Council (1975) field officer visited sixty-five small schools in twenty-nine LEAs in England and Wales in an exploratory survey of the problem. Three one-teacher schools and four four-teacher schools were included but the great majority were either two- or three-teacher schools. No information was available about the age of thirteen schools, but of the remainder, all but nine were built more than sixty years ago. At least eighteen were under consideration for closure. Resource provision generally was at a high level. A couple of schools were without a telephone and several lacked a playing field despite their location in the countryside, but almost all had a television, radio, tape recorder or gramophone, and library provision was often singled out for praise by the teachers. No analysis could be made of the running costs of these schools or of alternative schemes of organization. Nor was any attempt made to assess objectively the attainments of the pupils or the quality of the teaching, but the researcher did comment favourably on the generally high quality of education in these schools. Not all were of the same standard, but, as the field officer noted, this would be true of any random group of educational institutions. She observed that the teachers made a great contribution to the life of the community and commented, 'local communities have much to thank teachers in re-establishing social activities'. The teachers had different opinions about the problem of teaching two or three age groups in one classroom. Some welcomed the challenge and opportunities it offered, while others would have preferred to teach a single year group. There were different opinions, also, about the prospects for promotion. Some said that the idea had never occurred to them, while others were concerned that they might be overlooked. The most pressing difficulty seemed to be the problem of getting a supply teacher in staff absence. This made it almost impossible to attend in-service meetings. The field officer felt that the teacher's main problem was one of isolation; she noted how often teachers remarked how nice it was to see a new face. The survey concluded with an account of three schemes run by LEAs to give support to teachers in small and remote schools. This is a matter which will be more fully discussed in a later section. The Schools Council survey raises all the key issues: economic pressures, the quality of education and the need for special assistance. Each of these points is considered in turn by Nash (1977) in a report on rural primary schools in North Wales. The problems of cost head the list.

The costs of rural schools

There are districts where sufficient spare capacity exists to allow reorganization to take place without any expenditure on new buildings. This capacity may result from incompleted area school plans, from purpose-built all-age schools dating from the pre-war period and now used only for primary education, or simply from a natural decline in the number of children in the district. A detailed study of one area in North Wales where 503 pupils were taught in thirteen schools by thirty-four teachers suggests that the system could be reorganized without any capital expenditure by closing the six two-teacher schools and, in all, reducing by seven the number of teachers employed. The teacher–pupil ratio would rise from 15:1 to 19:1 but that would still be generous compared with urban school ratios. At 1975–6 prices the per capita cost would fall from £517 to £454. It is interesting to note that the number of children who would qualify for free transport would rise from 200 to 284, far less than might be expected, and additional transport costs would not begin to offset the savings to be gained by closing six schools. In fact, the LEA would make a saving of around 12.5 per cent on the annual running costs. This may not sound so great, but such a reorganization would withstand a further decline in the school population far more economically than the existing system. If the number of pupils fell by only 10 per cent to around 450 (an eventuality which will almost certainly occur), the number of teachers could be reduced to as few as twenty-two representing a further considerable economy. This type of reorganization, which can be effected piecemeal without additional building costs, is obviously attractive to LEAs: there is a case that resources are being wasted and that is hard to justify.

There is a classic example of area school replacement, one of the few for which data are available, near Tregaron in Dyfed. The Welsh Education Office report (1976) shows that five schools were closed (in 1975): Llangybi (built 1878) with thirty-six pupils and two teachers; Betws Bledrws (1830) with fifteen pupils and two teachers; Silian (1855) with eighteen pupils and two teachers; Cellan (1900) with eleven pupils and one teacher, and Llanfair Clydogau (1877) with nineteen pupils and two teachers. In 1975 the pupils were transferred to a new and well-equipped area community school. Even with seven teachers and a large transport bill, the area school is cheaper to run than the five old schools. The costs have had to be estimated, but, at 1976 prices, figures of around £71,000 for the five old schools and £54,000 for the area school are unlikely to be too far out. The running costs exclude the capital charges on the construction cost of £158,000. These charges are expensive and will remain a burden on the LEA for twenty years; if they are included, the economic benefits of the school look very marginal. There would certainly have been less costly forms of reorganization. The LEA might have considered closing the two smallest schools, maintaining two others (perhaps as Welsh-medium schools) with twenty-five pupils and two teachers each, and one (perhaps as an English-medium school) with forty to fifty pupils and three teachers. Some renovations would have been necessary to at least one of the schools, but the running costs would have been comparable with those of the new school. It is clear that area schools are not necessarily the most economic form of reorganization, even in the most ideal case.

There are instances when schools will have to be maintained no matter how small they become. There are areas of remote valleys where small settlements are six or seven miles from a larger village, and in such places it may be necessary to maintain a school with only one teacher and as few as ten to fifteen pupils. In North Wales there are a number of settlements like this, and it is evident from an examination of the map, that the closure of the isolated schools in that region could be achieved only at enormous social cost and perhaps with only slight financial benefits.

It is clear from this that one cannot talk loosely about the economic benefits of primary school reorganization in the countryside. Certainly it cannot be said that the area school is always the answer. Each individual case must be examined on its merits and a full costing of the various alternatives made.

Assessing the performance of small schools

There is a continual argument about the standards of education in small, as well as large, schools. It is one which cannot be resolved by objective or positivist research: we might say that one man's concentration on the basic subjects is another man's unbalanced curriculum. LEA officers sometimes find that parents see as good, and even outstanding, teachers those who are following what the officers regard as outmoded practices. In other words the criteria of assessment are subjective, and the question of who shall make them is, therefore, a crucial political question.

It has to be said that no reliable data relating to the attainments of children in small rural primary schools, compared with larger primary schools, are available. It is possible to pick up indications from National Foundation for Educational Research surveys, which suggest that standards of reading are certainly no lower in rural primary schools than in larger urban schools. Primary school size has never been identified by national surveys as a factor depressing attainment. During the course of our research in North Wales it was possible to show that, for a sample of more than 600 pupils in twenty-six rural schools, there were no significant differences between the attainments of pupils in the ten two-teacher schools and those in larger schools.

In fact, it is hard to find inspectors and advisers who will say that the quality of education in the two-teacher school is necessarily of lower quality than that provided by the larger school. They will say that it depends on the teacher. Where the teachers are hardworking and competent, the quality of the education will be high, but where they are not, the consequences of their lack of effort or competence will be much worse than in larger schools. In other words a large school can carry an inadequate teacher, but a two-teacher school cannot. In the opinion of many advisers the risk is not worth taking.

The whole business of assessing teachers is fraught with difficulties. Nevertheless, assessments have to be made by, among others, headteachers, advisers, HMIs and teaching practice supervisors. During the course of our research, after conversations with many advisers and adopting their criteria, we grouped the headteachers of twenty-six country schools into five categories.

Dedicated teachers

These are mostly mature teachers who have been in their post for some years. They have, for the most part, little interest in promotion and, in general, are thought to be over-traditional in their teaching methods and are unlikely to be considered for promotion in any case. The feel most at ease in their classroom with their children: teaching has become the central business of their lives.

Ambitious teachers

These are mostly young men and women in their thirties who see their present school as a stepping stone to a larger school in the forseeable future. Their aim is to make a visible success of their little school and they commonly introduce modern innovations, for example, open-plan, integrated day schemes, or independent learning programmes. The informal character of these classrooms is, in most cases, more apparent than real and the children are invariably required to work to a high standard.

Established teachers

These are teachers who have relinquished the idea of being further promoted and have accepted the position of village school teachers. It is an important role. The teacher becomes a community counsellor, he runs the village committees, and people regard him as a source of advice on a wide range of local matters. His school work settles into an established routine (he might himself admit that things have fallen into a rut) and advisers often regard the curriculum as unbalanced, but the basic subjects are well covered and the parents are more than satisfied.

Uninvolved teachers

There are teachers who, having perhaps failed one promotion interview too many, become a little bored and take up an all absorbing interest in something else. Such a teacher may find his major satisfactions in, for example, running a pottery or writing sermons as a lay preacher, but whatever it is, it takes first place in his life's plan. His school work is done between 9 a.m. and 3.30 p.m., and the pupils become accustomed to what he might refer to, if he had attended the LEAs in-service courses, as an independent learning programme.

64

Pre-retired teachers

There are some teachers who, having taught the same curriculum in the same schoolroom for twenty or thirty years, have retirement as their only life project. The curriculum is unimaginative, and the teaching uninspired. Unless the infants' teacher is willing and capable, the children do little but sit at their desks throughout the day – in some cases watching television for up to a third of their time in school.

There is some evidence, reported more fully in Nash (1977), that children in the classes of teachers categorized as dedicated attain higher than average reading scores and that pupils in the classes of teachers in the pre-retired category attain lower than average reading scores. These findings must be regarded as tentative but they support the common sense view that the small school is as good as the headteacher.

Helping small schools

The Schools Council (1975) survey reported three examples of specific LEA schemes to strengthen teaching in small schools. One LEA has organized periodic workshop sessions where headteachers can exchange ideas; another has appointed a specialist curriculum adviser to promote inter-school contact between teacher and pupils and to encourage the possibilities of joint educational activities; another has given the teachers' centres a particular responsibility for teachers in small remote schools. The teachers are reported to be enthusiastic about these attempts which at least display a concern for their problems. Cumbria's scheme, operating from the Wigton Teachers' Centre, is a particularly interesting example of the efforts being made. The desolate uplands near the Scottish border have suffered greatly from depopulation and loss of services in recent years, and the schools in this area have found the centre most useful as a focus for discussion and joint developments. The work of the centre will be discussed more fully in chapter 6. Cambridgeshire is now experimenting with a scheme under which two or three small schools will be regarded, for the purposes of staffing, as one unit and will be the responsibility of one headteacher. This is intended to establish continuing contact at all levels between the outlying schools and the base school and to permit a much greater flexibility of staffing, thus allowing teachers with specialist skills to work regularly with children in the outlying schools. Benford (1978) refers to the Oxfordshire mini-bus scheme which allows a group of eight or nine village schools access to a shared vehicle in their area. Other schemes have concentrated on in-service training. It is suggested that an annual four- or five-day course for teachers in remote areas, who are unable because of distance to reach a central teachers' centre, might be worthwhile in terms of the sustained enthusiasm and contacts which could be maintained throughout the year, even if the time had to be taken off the school year.

Many advisers view mobility of teachers in rural areas as a problem. There is increasing recognition of the need to redeploy headteachers who are no longer coping adequately with the task of running an isolated school. Resources are generally adequate, as the Schools Council paper pointed out, but there is a need for curriculum resources as well as teaching hardware. It is possible that a resource van, attached to a teachers' centre or educational technology centre and acting as a mobile library, would greatly add to the teaching power of a small school. Such a stock of resources, and an expert delivery system to make sure it is used, might greatly improve the quality of teaching in isolated schools. In certain curriculum areas in which teaching is known to be weak in rural schools, it might be worthwhile extending the idea to a mobile classroom, staffed by a specialist art or science teacher, for example, which could park in the school yard for a week, perhaps initiating a project which could be continued by the class teacher after the specialist mobile unit had departed. It has been suggested that the LEAs should have a clear policy and announce their reorganization schemes as early and as openly as possible. Many schools have lost pupils because parents, knowing that the school was under continual threat of closure, have preferred not to risk their children's education being disrupted and have sent them elsewhere.

The one-teacher school

The research at Bangor, reported in Nash *et al*. (1976), made a special study of five one-teacher schools, investigating the curriculum, the extent of the children's friendships, and costs. It was suggested that these small schools were able to provide a satisfactory education in most of the eight curriculum areas specified as appropriate for primary school children by the Gittins Report (1968). Only in the provision for team games was there a general weakness. The Gittins Report argued that children in small schools are deprived of the wider choice of friendships open to children in larger schools and that this might be detrimental to their social development. Nash *et al*. were able, in a detailed study of the three children in their sample who had no peer of their own sex or age (within a year), to show that, so far from the social development of these children being retarded, they, in fact, displayed considerable social maturity and their isolation was more apparent than real: their out-of-school social contacts were numerous, particularly so for the two locally born children who had kin in the district.

The costs of the schools were made available by the LEA and there is no escaping the conclusion that these schools were expensive to maintain. One school, chosen as the most representative in this respect, cost £6,624 in the financial year 1974–5 and, with fourteen pupils, the per capita cost was £473. This figure compares unfavourably with the 1972–3 Welsh average of £132. In another school with only eleven pupils the per capita cost rose to £848. This school was only a few miles from two larger villages both with good-sized schools and as the article pointed out:

> . . . it is understandable that the LEA should be tempted to take advantage of the huge saving that would be offered by closing [this school] and sharing the eleven pupils between the two three-teacher schools. If the children were split half and half no new cost, apart from taxi fares, need be incurred. The existing teacher–pupil ratios in the three-teacher schools are reasonably generous, and the marginal cost of educating a few extra pupils would be very low until the schools reached capacity.

The research also attempted to study the way in which these small schools contributed to the community's social existence and to its sense of identity. It seems that the attachment parents and other villagers in these communities had for their schools (two had fought successful campaigns to keep their schools open) is related to the fundamental function of the school as an agent in the continuity of village life. It is seen not only as an educational institution but as a symbol of the community's commitment to its future. The loss of the school is thus seen as a contributory factor in the decline of Welsh rural society and its distinctive culture. The research concluded:

> The case for closing the very small schools has been made many times by powerful spokesmen. It is true that they are expensive to run, it is true that they cannot teach certain subjects – notably physical education – as well as can larger schools, it is true that a teacher working alone has little opportunity to attend in-service training courses except during vacations and that her work can suffer from the effects of her isolation. But closing down the schools seems a particularly drastic solution to these problems. For the successes of these small schools are far more impressive than their failures. Their pupils are respected as people in their own right – their presence in the school is noticeably valued – they attain a perfectly satisfactory standard in academic and in most non-academic areas of the curriculum. The relations between teachers and the parents are close, the school provides an emotional focus for the community and, in many cases, an actual meeting place. We believe that the school of one teacher plus a nursery assistant with between 15–25 children is a viable and satisfactory type of school for the small rural community.

Summary and conclusion

There has never been a time when village schools have not been under the threat of closure. Declining population, the loss of the senior group to the secondary school, educational concerns expressed by Plowden and Gittins, economic difficulties and renewed pressure from central government now that the falling rolls resulting from the decline in family size have begun to be felt, have all steadily reduced the number of village schools. The remarkable feature of the present phase is that the decisions of the professional LEA staff are being challenged by local protest groups.

My own research in North Wales provides the only published analysis of the educational, social and economic viability of rural primary schools. It cannot be regarded as conclusive but will, at least, supplement LEA studies which are generally not available for public discussion.

The present Organization for Economic Co-operation and Development (OECD) study of educational provision in sparsely populated areas will add a new dimension to the debate. It is already known that in several other European countries the trend of school closures has been reversed. In Ireland, the government is now committed to maintain small country schools and in Norway and Finland several schools closed in the 1960s have been re-opened. New Zealand has also reversed its policy of consolidating rural primary schools. In these countries it has been realized that the educational benefits of larger schools are illusory and that the policy has caused real hardship to individuals and actual damage to the viability and structure of rural communities.

5

Secondary schooling

Coming at a time when the DES apparently still favours large secondary schools, the sharp decline in school enrolments, referred to in the previous chapter, is likely to cause some strain in the smaller rural schools. The widespread adoption of comprehensive education in the 1960s saw the closure of many smaller secondary modern schools, which had been provided after the war in some of the larger villages, and the organization of rural secondary education in the market towns. Villagers have become accustomed to sending their children to town secondary schools and in most areas there is little scope for further secondary school reorganization. The relevant questions of the organizational effects of school size, the relationship between school size and pupil achievement, and the provision of a broader curriculum through alternative teaching methods will be the subject of this chapter.

Secondary school provision

Secondary education came late to the rural areas. In 1961 there

70

were still 1,026 all-age schools – almost all in rural areas – with more than 37,000 pupils. Some rural counties, Anglesey is a particular example, responded early to the need to provide secondary education to their underpopulated districts by introducing fully comprehensive schemes. Others, like Montgomeryshire, preferred to maintain their grammar school provision intact and build a number of small secondary modern schools.

The recommendations of Circular 144 (1947) for a minimum entry of 300–500 pupils (i.e. a school of 1,600–1,700) were reinforced by Circular 10/65 (1965) which recommended a minimum entry of 180–200 pupils and envisaged schools with a total roll beyond 2,000. Much of this thinking was based on the now discredited IQ-based theory that 70 per cent of the child population did not have the necessary intellectual capacity for sixth form work. But, whatever the ideal size might be in official thinking, there was no choice but to accept small comprehensive schools in the rural counties – and there are a large number of such schools. The official statistics do not allow urban–rural differences to be discerned easily, but figures on the size of schools are available. In 1975 there were 8 schools with up to 100 pupils on roll, 51 between 101–200, 130 between 201–300, and 227 between 301–400. It is also possible to calculate that the average size of school – implying that there are many smaller – in a sample of predominantly rural counties, was 590 in Northumberland, 639 in Norfolk and 641 in Cumbria.

Benn and Simon (1970) show that of 728 comprehensive schools in England and Wales at that time, 100 (14 per cent) were sited either in villages with a population of less than 5,000 or in the countryside. These schools had a greater proportion of higher ability pupils than comprehensive schools in suburbs, towns or cities. Their average sixth form size was sixty. A further forty-four schools were sited in larger towns but also accepted children from the surrounding countryside. They, too, had a high proportion of higher ability pupils. Their average sixth form size was seventy-one.

The effects of school size

Most of the work on the effects of size on organization has been done by researchers working in institutions other than schools – in offices and workshops and so on – but there is no reason to believe that schools are likely to be unaffected by the processes found to be important in these studies. The general conclusion is that, other things being equal, small organizations are more efficient than large organizations. Campbell (1970), for example, reports that persons in smaller institutions are more punctual, more productive, are absent less often and are less likely to resign. Just as importantly, they find themselves more frequently in posts of responsibility, take part in a wider range of activities, have a broader conception of their role and participate in voluntary activities more readily. In schools it is safe to conclude that, as size increases, teachers know a smaller proportion of the total number of pupils. According to Halsall (1973), control outside the classroom is at least three times as difficult in fourteen-form entry schools as in three-form entry schools, and at most nine times more difficult.

Perhaps the best known study of school size is that carried out by Barker and Gump (1964) who studied the range of behavioural settings in a sample of Kansas High Schools ranging in size from 35 to 2,287 students. Their ecological perspective makes it difficult to relate their work to other research, particularly as most of their attention is paid to non-classroom settings. The essential findings of their study are best expressed in their own words:

> . . . small high schools are, in fact, not so small on the inside as they are on the outside. In terms of number of behaviour settings, number of characteristics per setting – interior characteristics not easily seen from the outside – small schools differ less from large schools than in terms of number of students and amount of space, which are perceptually salient external attributes of schools.

Students in small schools were under more pressure to participate and felt a greater sense of responsibility and obligation. The authors were in no doubt that students in these schools led a much more satisfying life than those in larger colleges.

72

In Britain, Monks' (1968) research for the NFER included a special study of four rural schools which showed that there was a high level of interest and participation by all pupils in extra-curricular activities. In the urban schools there was a significant tendency for working-class pupils to have a lower level of participation which was not evident in the rural schools. In the rural schools, 27 per cent of pupils took no part in such activities, 23 per cent took part in one activity only and 51.1 per cent took part in two or more activities. In the urban schools, the figures were 46 per cent, 25 per cent and 29 per cent respectively. As Monks points out, the urban schools were about twice the size of the rural schools and this may well have been more important that their geographical location.

Very little research has concerned itself with the attainments of pupils educated in secondary schools of different sizes. In Britain, Monks' work is probably most relevant. Where rural and urban children were compared, the rural children were generally superior in attainments to their urban contemporaries. The average score (aggregated from a variety of suitable attainment tests) of first year pupils in a sample of rural schools was 76.5 compared with 74.7 for a similar group of pupils in a sample of urban schools. In the fourth year the scores were 101.7 and 99.3 and in the sixth year 56.7 and 51.7 respectively. All these differences were statistically significant. When analysed by school size the same general pattern of differences was found in favour of small schools. Schools of 600 or less had average first year scores of 75.5 compared with 72.7 in schools of 1,201 and over, at fourth year average scores were 103.4 compared with 97.2, and at sixth year 55.7 compared with 49.3. The quality of the analysis in Monks' work leaves much to be desired and it is impossible to say whether the results have been greatly affected by other factors. Some city comprehensives are creamed by competing grammar schools (this is certainly true of the largest group of comprehensive schools in this sample which are all within the ILEA area). Equally important, often no allowance has been made for social class differences, and where class is taken into account the analysis is seriously deficient. For example, all farmers, farm managers, market gardeners, etc., are included in the same non-manual grouping regardless of size of holding. This must seriously over-represent the size of the non-manual group in the rural sample.

Others who have examined the relationship between school size and performance have been equally unconvinced of the meaningful nature of the trivial differences that can be found. Halsall (1973) believes that the relationship is not proven and finds the research contradictory and confusing – a view that is confirmed by the findings of the NFER research by Ross *et al*. (1972). David (1976), who has reviewed this area of research, concludes that large schools make very little difference to educational outcomes but happen to be a convenient weapon with which to fight other battles. She writes:

> I believe that the problem posed is false: size is not an independent variable affecting the outcomes of schooling and school organization. It is a mediating variable between purposes and effects of education. The problem posed neglects the essential fact that size cannot be divorced from context. Indeed, even if an optimal size could be established the change from inappropriate to appropriate size would produce unanticipated effects. The relationships would not remain constant. This issue, however, has been completely ignored in the debates.

Curriculum provision

Halsall (1973) has been responsible for the most systematic analysis of the viability of the small comprehensive school in terms of its ability to provide an adequate curriculum for pupils of all ages and abilities. She shows that a two-form entry school of about 200 pupils can meet the basic curriculum requirements up to and including fifth form level. One existing school of this size offers CSE/GCE up to twelve subjects. She regards the smallest viable 11–18 comprehensive school as a four-form entry school of 400–600 pupils. One such school on the Isle of Man offers sixteen A–levels out of nineteen subjects taken in the sixth form. Halsall writes:

> . . . the relationship between size of school and validity of the sixth form does not merely depend on the size of the school,

as was thought in the early days of comprehensive education, but also on the average size of class and on the numbers staying on in the sixth form.

She describes in considerable detail how existing small comprehensive schools in rural areas do manage to offer an adequate curriculum. One three-form entry school, for example, offers physics, chemistry, mathematics, biology, geography, history, French, English and arranges art in another school for pupils who opt for it. The four-form entry school has more flexibility and can offer a choice of options suitable for non-academic pupils. There is no doubt that it can provide a curriculum leading ultimately to a wide range of university courses for the minority and give a good general education for the majority. Her analysis shows that such a school can offer eleven or twelve A–levels, without the need to teach the upper and lower sixth together (except occasionally for some laboratory work), as well as allowing for split classes in maths and in music or domestic science, and for O–level repeats in the sixth form. Moreover, this can be achieved with only four of the thirty staff needing to teach more than one subject. There are various administrative measures which can be used to broaden the subject range of small schools, notably subject sharing with neighbouring schools and joint courses with technical colleges which are already extensively practised by some small schools in rural areas.

Halsall points out that 80 per cent of the sixth form subjects are covered by eight A–levels: English, French, history, geography, mathematics, physics, chemistry and biology. Together with seven other subjects the coverage is 97 per cent. If a three-form entry school can provide ten A–levels – and some existing ones do – then there doesn't seem much to worry about. There is a need to see that peripheral A–levels are provided for in some way and that the needs of the majority, the non-academic sixth form, for commercial and technical subjects are adequately covered; however, both theoretical studies and the experience of existing schools show clearly that the small school can provide a curriculum at all levels of the modern comprehensive school.

75

Independent learning and technology

The use of independent learning, whether technology-based or not, has obvious attractions for small schools. Halsall (1973) points out that the criteria governing their use of independent learning schemes must be threefold:

1 Are they as effective as a teacher?
2 Are they more or less expensive to install or operate than a full or part time teacher?
3 Is enough material available to justify their substantial use?

In England and Wales there are two major non-profit-making correspondence colleges, offering O– and A–levels in addition to a wide variety of technical and commercial courses, which are already used to some extent by small comprehensive schools. Halsall has calculated that if every small comprehensive school was allowed a minimum of five correspondence A–levels, then that number of pupils would have the opportunity to choose a subject outside the official provision and, since even the smallest of these schools can manage eleven or twelve A–levels, this would allow sixteen or seventeen A–level choices, or 97 per cent of all A–levels taken by sixth-form students. Educational radio and television appear to offer useful possibilities, and the Open University has made these media an integral part of its teaching, but, at school level, programmes are aimed at supervised class groups and there has been little use of its potential for independent learning. Language laboratories are probably the best known of the recent attempts to bring technology-based learning into the schools. As languages are likely to be one of the areas where there will be a narrowing of course options in small schools, independent learning may become particularly important in this field. It has been shown that a school which provides programmed course material in a language laboratory can extend its range beyond the skills of existing staff.

A substantial body of experience has been built up in computer education through the involvement of the National Council for Educational Technology in a £2½ million project in computer-assisted learning. None of the many research projects was concerned with rural schools (indeed a great deal of the research was not located in schools at all but in technical and military colleges). However, one project at school level has been directly concerned with small groups of pupils. CAMOL (computer managed physics scheme) is used by 150 pupils in Belfast and by 80 in Birmingham, where it is used by several small sixth forms in consortia. The computer is employed as an aid in assessing the pupils' performance, to keep a record of their progress, to advise students of their route through the structured course, to report on performance to students and teachers and to report on the quality of the tests. The project has not been finally evaluated but does suggest numerous possibilities for further developments.

A similar independent learning course has been developed for use in Inner London Education Authority schools. ILEA comprehensive schools are not small but in the early 1970s they were desperately short of qualified physics teachers and independent learning seemed a possible solution. Work on APPIL (Advanced Physics Project for Independent Learning) began in 1975 at the South London Science Centre. The course is designed for those pupils (the majority) who have studied traditional O–level physics, rather than the integrated Nuffield course, and is, therefore, traditional in its approach. It consists of ten units covering three broad themes in physics. Six of these units are studied in the first year of the course and four in the second year, and there is a considerable element of freedom in choosing the sequence of units. Although the students work independently, they are not unsupervised, and tutors are available at frequent and regular intervals, especially for practical work. The course team and the teachers working with the materials have been strongly influenced by Open University practices, and considerable efforts have been made to specify learning objectives, to build in self-assessment procedures and to create a highly structured learning programme. Between early 1976 and 1978, the materials had been used in more than fifty schools, although not all have been involved with the project and its materials to the same degree. Schools varied in the number of pupils taking the course from one or two to more than twenty. Some schools adopted the scheme in its entirety, while others made use of selected items only. In some schools, pupils have given students study time without supervision (although with a teacher on call in most cases); others have had a tutor timetabled for all sessions. Schools have been encouraged to co-operate at sixth-form level, thus allowing expensive items of equipment to be shared and, incidentally, helping to counteract the lack of stimulus individuals working in very small groups might have otherwise experienced.

Bauser (1978), the project director, writes: 'APPIL has shown that "independent learning" or "resource-based" learning not only can go a long way to solve the problems of small A–level groups, but has advantages which make it applicable much more generally.' No figures are available for the number of pupils who have successfully achieved A–levels through this scheme – and since schools have varied considerably in the extent to which they have made use of the materials the figures might not be particularly meaningful – but it is generally considered successful. There is only minimal computer involvement at present but there are several possible developments, including a branching programme by which a pupil could obtain revision material or more advanced work depending on his needs. Interest in independent learning schemes of this sort is strong in science, perhaps because it readily lends itself to the linear, hierarchical and heavily structured presentation of subject matter which characterizes current programmed learning schemes. There is, however, insufficient evidence to enable firm statements to be made about the potential future role of technology-based learning in small secondary schools. Low technology packages like APPIL are encouraging but everything suggests that CAI (Computer Aided Instruction) and CML (Computer Managed Learning) are now, and will remain for the next decade at least, an additional cost to educational budgets and cannot be used as major alternatives to teachers. In this respect they are tools for teacher use and are no different from audio-visual aids, or for that matter print libraries; they cost more but they do offer the possibilities of improved teaching.

Project PHI

Only one British project has been entirely concerned with the development of independent learning in rural secondary schools – Project Highlands and Islands. It is worth discussing at some length for two reasons: first, its various reports have not been published in a readily available form, and second, its methodological implications are at least as important as its substantive findings.

Until the mid-1960s, when secondary education was reorganized in Scotland, ordinary secondary schools catered merely for those children who were not awarded places in the selective schools. After reorganization, a decision had to be made about the future of the very small schools. The question was whether they should be closed and the pupils provided with transport to, or boarding places in, larger schools, or to retain the schools and provide them with new resources based on developments in educational technology thus enabling them to teach as successfully as large schools. Project PHI was established to study the possibilities of the latter approach. In 1970 the project conducted a survey of the use of audio-visual equipment in Highland and Island schools, developed multi-media materials for use with the new Scottish Integrated Science Scheme, and evaluated their use in thirty-three rural schools. Roebuck *et al*. (1974), after research with the Ministry of Overseas Development, recognized that the effectiveness of programmed materials was dependent upon the response of the teachers using the materials and that success depended as much on the administrative stability of the school, and the teachers' confidence in the materials, as on the intrinsic quality of the materials themselves. Project PHI thus attempted to develop materials to support rather than replace the teacher or to change his role.

The initial survey showed that the schools had a relatively low use of audio-visual equipment. For example, over the period of a fortnight, 29.8 per cent of schools had used a duplicator, 24 per cent a tape recorder, 21 per cent a slide or film strip projector, 7 per cent a television receiver, 6.7 per cent a radio set and 4 per cent an 8mm film projector. The project team thus decided to develop materials which would require the use of only film strip projectors and tape recorders. Individualized learning materials, suitable for use by groups or pairs of children, were designed in consultation with teachers and HMIs and test trials of the materials were run before final production. Despite problems associated with staff changes on the project team and an acute shortage of funds, the materials were produced and disseminated to the schools where they were used by over 2,000 pupils. The evaluation procedure provided data suitable for numerical analysis and records of observations and interviews which could be used to illuminate in a less rigorous fashion the results of the project. Participant observation was carried out in five schools and half of the teachers involved were interviewed. The thirty-three schools in the study comprised 44 per cent of the secondary schools in the five Highland and Island counties and ranged in size from below 50 pupils (fourteen schools) to over 400 pupils (two schools). The largest single group of schools were those which provided only non-certificate courses and part O–grade. Just three schools were fully comprehensive in providing a course to sixth-form level. The class size for first year science groups ranged from three to twenty-seven, the median size being sixteen. All the schools had a science teacher, although three of these thought of themselves as mathematicians rather than scientists. The mean allocation for science was 4.5 periods of 40 minutes, but the range varied widely from 1.8 to 6.12 periods a week. Physical provision was reasonable; all had electricity and gas supply, twenty-eight had permanent hot water and 9 per cent had a preparation room.

Despite the close involvement of the teachers at all stages of the project, there is strong evidence to suggest that they were not looking for structured learning materials of the kind the project was producing. When asked how best to improve science teaching, the teachers placed the greatest importance on developing closer contact with colleagues in other schools and on more flexible procedures for ordering equipment. Only a small majority were influenced by developments in educational technology, and most taught in a traditional way using textbooks and teacher demonstrations with pupil experiments. An indication of the impact of the project can be gained from the extent of follow-up interest. At the end of the first year of trials twenty-five of the thirty-three schools replied to an invitation to re-use the materials: seventeen requested the tape-slide sequences, eighteen the worksheets and twenty the end-of-year test. The tape-slide sequences were the most popular but were seen as a supplementary resource not as a replacement. The experiences the teachers had with the project did not result in altered patterns of teaching, and the form of the materials was not seen as a model for restructuring their own course, except in a small minority of cases.

An attempt was made at a quantitive analysis of the relationship between the project materials and pupil attainments. Apparently, the distance of the school from the county office had about the same degree of impact on attainment as the materials, and it was quite impossible to reach wholly satisfactory conclusions about the value of the project using this mode of analysis alone. It is worth noting that, with the exception of the junior secondary schools, the quality of teaching and level of resources were as adequate in these remote schools as in the rest of Scotland. It is clear that any differences were due to size not location. Where numbers were high enough to allow year grouping (i.e. single-form entry or 150–200 pupils) small schools could follow the existing syllabus just as well as larger schools. Effectiveness of the syllabus was shown to be more related to the provision of materials and staffing levels than to location, and in this respect the materials were as relevant to large urban schools as to small rural schools where exactly the same factors would qualify their success.

Three years after the project started, four of the five counties adopted a two-tier comprehensive system. Pupils remained in the primary school for a two-year secondary course before being transferred to the high school at fourteen. This policy made more funds available to teachers and schools so that by the time PHI materials had been developed the pedagogical problems which prompted their development had ceased to exist: the schools were no longer ill-equipped and poorly staffed. Moreover, the integrated Scottish General Science syllabus (physics, chemistry, biology) proved to be fortuitously well suited to the small school where departmental rivalries were no barrier to its implementation and where the mixed-ability

81

methods it was designed for were likely to be most appropriate. In this connection Hamilton (1973), who worked on the project, comments:

> In many countries it is assumed that rural schools are qualitatively different from their urban counterparts. In Scotland this is certainly true with regard to small schools. Nevertheless it does not follow that these differences can be equated with deficiencies. Even using recognized criteria (e.g., qualifications of teaching staff, and the proportion of children remaining at school beyond the statutory leaving age), the secondary schools in the Highlands and Islands are above average when compared with all Scottish local authority schools. Indeed, the county with the highest percentage of 18-year-olds at school (Shetland) is also the most remote.

Summary and conclusion

The relationship between school size and educational quality proves as difficult to establish for secondary schools as for primary schools. The recommended minimum size of 1,600–1,700 is rarely attained by comprehensive schools in the rural areas. About 20 per cent of comprehensives are sited either in the countryside or in small towns with rural catchment areas. Their average size is around 600–50 pupils, and their sixth forms, with an average of 60–70 pupils, compare favourably with urban comprehensives. The few studies available suggest that only trivial differences exist between the attainment level of pupils in large and small, and urban and rural schools; those which have been found invariably favour small rural schools. The experience of the smallest existing schools shows that the four-form entry, 11–18 years school, of 450–600 pupils can provide an adequate O– and A–level coverage and meet the needs of non-academic pupils for vocational options. It is apparent that innovations in educational technology and independent learning have had, as yet, but a slight impact on the secondary schools. Some small schools do use correspondence courses, but there is considerable reluctance to give independent learning more than a very minor position in the school system. The ILEA physics project (APPIL) is, in this respect, a particularly interesting development and could well be extended to provide minority A–levels in schools of all sizes. The possibilities of independent learning in languages are equally neglected, although the benefits of being able to offer additional languages are obvious. The computer revolution has not affected the schools to any substantial extent. Very little of the huge sums of research money have gone into independent learning projects, and only one of these is concerned (and then only contingently) with small sixth forms. For at least the next decade it seems that computer-managed learning will remain an add-on cost and, therefore, of little use to small schools looking for extra teaching capacity. Although the original objective of project PHI – to provide small ill-equipped and poorly staffed schools with the means to teach science – was made redundant by organizational changes, there are many lessons to be learnt from the project's history. The inadequacy of the conventional methods of assessing changes in teaching and learning are evident enough. It is worth noting, in passing, that no differences associated with the urban and rural location of the schools could be found, but the important message is that change lies in the hands of the teachers and cannot be imposed by outside workers, no matter how enlightened their intentions. The great majority of science teachers involved with the project did not adopt independent learning techniques but simply sucked in the project materials as an additional resource within the context of their established teaching patterns. This may have been for the best.

6

Education and rural-based minority cultures

In chapter 1 it was argued that the occupation of rural sociologists was the study of the relationship between the economically powerful urban centres and the less-developed rural periphery. Accepting this enables us to see rural-based minority cultures in a new perspective. The school system has been seen both as a major instrument in the assimilation of such minorities into the dominant national culture and as a means of maintaining their distinctive values. The education of rural minorities is thus a relevant concern in the study of rural education.

There are two lines of approach: through work in ethnicity and through work in bilingualism. Although these have been carved up as separate fields of academic study and have developed their own theoretical concepts, there are encouraging signs, for example in Giles (1977) and Bourhis *et al*. (1973), of their reintegration. Before discussing their work it is necessary to show how the two specialities have taken parallel paths.

Ethnicity

Research into ethnicity has, until recently, been dominated by the so-called 'inductive typology mode', of which Schermerhorn (1970) is the best know exponent, with its stress on the integration of ethnic groups derived from a structural functionalist theory of social processes. In Barth's (1959) view the genesis and persistence of ethnic boundaries and the organization of inter-ethnic relations are seen to be related to factors affecting the competition for environmental resources. Ethnicity is further regarded as self-ascribed and based on criteria of territoriality (or nationality), common notions of descent, language (or speech modes) and religion. All have, or in the case of language are, attributes of presentation which are perceived intersubjectively to generate sufficiently clear boundaries. In Barth's view, only one of these four criteria are necessary to create a consciousness of ethnicity amongst a population. But, in order for such a consciousness to arise, it is further necessary for a group to be engaged in a power relationship with others, so that boundaries are marked and attributes of presentation become functional. Thus, ethnic consciousness can occur with equal probability in a geographically isolated group or in a stratified society where social isolation has been imposed. Bell (1974), reporting the Social Science Research Council conference on ethnicity, gives the following definition: 'It was proposed that ethnicity (1) involves a past-orientated group identification emphasizing origins; (2) includes some conception of cultural and social distinctiveness; and (3) relates to a component unit in a broader system of social relations.' The conceptualization of ethnicity as a largely subjective process of status identification according to these criteria has not been wholly accepted by writers who wish to retain an objective view of cultural behaviour, but the Barthian model is now probably the dominant perspective.

Sociologists could hardly have overlooked the connection between ethnicity and social competition for resources. The concept of ethnic division of labour, so obviously applicable to that form of social organization practised in South Africa, is commonly employed in American studies with reference to the position of Black, Puerto Rican and other identifiable ethnic groups who occupy low status positions in the American economy. The term 'internal colonialism' has been used to describe the relationship which obtains when an ethnic division of labour coexists with geographical segregation. Again, South Africa's so called Bantustans are the paradigm case; but the concept has had wide application. Hechter's (1975) work, which accounts for the relationship between England and Wales in these terms, has been hotly disputed but remains a good introduction to the theory. Williams (1978) and other critics of Hechter do not dispute the economic dependency of Wales or that it can be regarded as an internal colony, but argue that ethnic differences have little, if any, relevance. They show that although Wales is economically depressed in comparison with the rest of Britain, its urban areas are not so much more depressed than the North East, and its rural areas not so much more depressed than the South West regions of England. In their view, the economic dominance of the South East has resulted in the depression of Wales and of the outlying English regions. (See chapter 9 for further discussion.)

Bilingualism

Since the primary identifying characteristics of such ethnic minorities in most, but not all, cases is language, most of the work in education has been done in the field of bilingualism. Fishman (1976) draws attention to the way in which American schools, which played such an important part in the de-ethnicization of non-English-speaking immigrants to the USA in the last century, have begun to face the continuing existence of languages other than English in the USA. Fishman relates this to the growth of black consciousness which acted as a trigger for Mexican-Americans, Puerto Ricans, Native Americans (American Indians), Polish Americans and so on who have all asked for teaching in their own language. Fishman regards bilingual education as beneficial not only to the minority group but also to majority group in providing them with an insight into another cultural perspective. He gives a brief review of bilingual education in 110 nations and concludes that there is no sound evidence to suggest that bilingual education is in any respect inferior to monoglot education.

> All in all . . . I foresee only a small possible diminution in the total number of mother tongues by the year 2000 or by other foreseeable dates. Freisian- and Catalan- and Breton- and Basque- and Yiddish-speaking mothers are likely to continue to feel and believe that their mother tongues are as good and as beautiful and as inimitable – at least for everyday use with their children, husbands, and grandmothers – as do mothers who speak Albanian, Afrikaans or Hebrew.

Fishman's list here is no more than an arbitrary sampling. In addition to his own review, mentioned above, Stephens (1976) and Grant (1977) give an account of minority languages in Europe and the degree of recognition each receives in the educational system, and a report of the Centre for Information on Language Teaching and Research (1976) has a comprehensive report on the situation in Britain.

A socio-economic approach to ethnicity

The theoretical relationships between ethnicity, language use and aspirations for cultural and national recognition are being explored by a number of socio-linguists. The contribution of Giles (1977) is important, and several other writers, notably Yancey *et al*. (1976), have explored the conditions under which ethnicity and its chief marker – language – becomes important in political terms. Wirth (1954) delineated four distinct positions which subordinate groups may adopt towards the majority culture:

1 Assimilation, a desire to merge into the dominant group and consequently reject their own cultural attributes;
2 Pluralism, a wish to coexist as equal partners in the national community;
3 Secessionism, a desire to break free of the political and cultural control of the dominant group; and
4 Militancy, a wish to overthrow the dominance of the majority group and replace it with their own.

87

These positions will be found useful in the discussion which follows.

Surprisingly little is known about such basic processes as language maintenance and change in communities and individuals, and even less about the importance or otherwise of formal education in these processes. On the one hand we have seen, in special circumstances, the adoption of Hebrew (regarded a few years ago as a dead language) as the common tongue of modern Israel. But, in the same period, attempts to reintroduce Irish have failed despite, according to MacNamara (1966), an estimated ten hours of primary school instruction a week. Given the present state of theoretical development it is perhaps more useful, at this stage, to analyse the conditions affecting the education of specific linguistic minorities.

There is little point in attempting a survey of bilingual education programmes or a comparative study of ethnic relations in these pages, and it seems sensible to limit the following discussion to these shores. In Britain there are two indigenous minorities, the Welsh in Wales and the Gaels in Western Scotland, and the study of the development of education for those peoples will show the relevance of the theoretical points above. We may note at once that the very fact that the Welsh are confined to their present narrow boundaries on the westernmost fringe of the land, the result of the weakness of their sixth- and seventh-century chieftains against the might of the Saxon kings, is testimony enough to the importance of resource competition in ethnic relations!

Education in Wales and the Welsh language

In earlier chapters a little of the history of education in Wales was given: how the nonconformist stress on Bible reading led to the circulating schools of Griffith Jones and to the emergence of the Welsh as one of the first literate peoples of Europe. During the nineteenth century the provision of education in Wales followed the English pattern with the National Society of the Established Church and the nonconformist British and Foreign Schools Society. Both provided an English-medium education in contrast to the Sunday schools (which had continued the work of the circulating schools) where instruction was in Welsh. The central government in England was conscious of the power of education in easing the threat of social disturbance in the depressed areas of Wales, and in 1839 the member for Coventry told the House of Commons: 'It should be borne in mind that an ill-educated and undisciplined population, like that existing amongst the mines in South Wales, is one that may be found most dangerous to the neighbourhood in which it dwells, and that a band of efficient schoolmasters is kept up at a much less expense than a body of soldiers.' As a result of this parliamentary debate, a report was commissioned on the condition of education in Wales. The final report (House of Commons, 1847) was so insulting that even today it can hardly be discussed dispassionately by Welsh writers. For example, of the school at Pandy Tudor, Denbighshire, the commissioners wrote:

> The master is 23 years of age; he has spent a month at a British School in North Wales, and attempts to imitate the British system. But some of his scholars surpassed him, both in respect of attainments and manners. His questions were slowly conceived such as might be expected from a child who had received an ordinary education. He understands English imperfectly, and in catechizing his pupils spoke incorrectly: e.g. 'Where River Thames *is*?' 'What Jesus Christ *did*?' etc. There was great confusion in the classification of his school; the discipline was not good; the children were exceedingly rude and unmannerly.

This young man was John Price who taught at Pandy Tudor for forty-seven years. He was to a considerable extent responsible for the education of Sir Henry Jones, a renowned scholar, and made an immense contribution to the well-being of the locality where he is still remembered as a good and cultured man.

The attitude of the commissioners, their hostility to the language, their contempt for Welsh literary and musical culture, their dismissal of the values of the Welsh people – which is evident in every page of the report – reflected the attitude of the central authorities towards Wales throughout the nineteenth century. Wales was treated by the authorities as if it were part of England and, when in 1862 the system of payment by results was introduced, Welsh was not, of course, included as an examinable subject. Since it did not pay teachers to use Welsh, they forbade it. A piece of wood which hung around the neck by a length of string, known as the 'Welsh Not', was given by the teacher to the first child in the class to speak Welsh – one word was enough – and he would hand it to anyone else he heard speaking Welsh. At the end of the day the unfortunate possessor of the 'Not' was beaten. There are many documented cases of this technique and its use was widespread. The 1870 Education Act completed the provision of elementary schooling in the rural areas of Wales but, although the schools were under the control of locally-elected school boards, they were still dependent upon grants awarded in proportion to the number of pupils successfully examined by HMIs and unable, even if willing, to introduce the teaching of Welsh. In 1893 it was permitted to teach certain subjects in Welsh in Welsh-speaking areas, but there was no real change in attitude until the formation of the Welsh Department of the Board of Education in 1907. At this time an influential, though minority, section of the Welsh middle class had become alarmed at the decline of the Welsh language and of the nonconformist values which had become associated with it. The new board was sympathetic to the Welsh language and, through its Inspectors, encouraged the use of Welsh as a medium of instruction in certain subjects, for example, history, geography, music, and nature study. Welsh was also permitted as a medium of instruction in infant classes where the pupils did not speak English.

From 1840 to 1893 Welsh had been excluded from the schools of Wales, even though for the last twenty years of that period the schools had been the responsibility of the local communities. It seems that the people accepted schooling in English in the belief that it was necessary for their children to learn English and that, since Welsh was learned in the home and was the common speech of the area, its exclusion from the school posed no threat to its survival.

English-medium elementary education was widespread in Wales by the 1850s, but secondary education was almost completely neglected. Thirty years later the Welsh elite had successfully gained three university colleges – Aberystwyth 1880,

Cardiff 1883 and Bangor 1884 – but it soon proved impossible to find a sufficient number of adequately prepared Welsh students. The old grammar schools had declined in importance and had no more than a handful of pupils (Llanrwst, for example, had thirty-six in 1884) and, though there were a number of proprietory or independent schools, there were no public schools of the type that had by then become successful in England. As a result of the 1889 Aberdare enquiry set up to investigate this problem, the Welsh Intermediate Education Act was passed giving the new county councils the power to take over the old grammar schools and establish new ones. These county schools were examined by the Central Welsh Board of Education, established for the purpose in 1896. Most of these schools were renamed grammar schools after the introduction of the central schools (non-academic secondary schools built following the Hadow report) from 1936 onwards.

In the county schools the curriculum was, in the early days, entirely academic – Latin, Greek, French, English, history, geography, scripture and mathematics. Evans (1974) shows that although the 1889 Act enabled the schools to teach a wide variety of subjects including commercial arithmetic, shorthand and bookkeeping and excluded only trade or industrial training, commercial subjects were rarely included. The over-academic nature of the curriculum was obvious even to contemporaries. Soon after it was created, the Welsh Department of the Board of Education criticized the lack of provision for biology and related agricultural subjects and the almost total neglect of the Welsh language. It blamed the Central Welsh Board's rigid examination system for the 'wooden and unintelligent type of mind' its own inspectors ritually complained of in their annual reports. The Welsh Department of the Board of Education had, however, more success in gaining recognition for Welsh than in widening the curriculum to include non-university subjects. But gradually, science, in the form of physics and chemistry, was added and in the 1920s commercial bookkeeping and shorthand writing became common. The schools (which were permitted under the Act to teach Welsh only as a *foreign* language) made more provision for Welsh, and the subject made steady progress. In 1897 only 31 of the 79 schools offered Welsh, but the proportion had risen to 96 out of 116 by 1925. Nowhere, though, was Welsh used as a medium of instruction and there was no suggestion that it should be. In a report of the inspection of Llanrwst in 1933, the HMI with responsibility for modern languages suggested that the pupils might be permitted to translate initially from French to Welsh in recognition that the grammatical similarities between Welsh and French might facilitate their understanding. There is no evidence that this suggestion was adopted.

There is no question that throughout the first half of this century the Welsh middle class saw grammar or county school education as a source of social and geographical mobility: a way out of the depressed industrial and agricultural valleys of Wales. The Welsh language had come to be seen as a handicap to personal advancement and as an indication of inferior status, and many middle-class and aspiring middle-class parents killed the language in their family by speaking only English to their children. There was no widespread or significant demand for Welsh-medium education at this time or for a greater recognition of Welsh in the schools or in the other social institutions of Wales. The University Colleges also adopted this position. To this day only a small number of courses are available through the medium of Welsh, ability to speak Welsh is not a condition of appointment and no particular encouragement is given to non-Welsh speakers who wish to learn the language.

By the 1950s it was possible to note a change in the attitude of the Welsh-speaking middle class. Khleif (1975, 1978) compares the growing ethnic consciousness and recent political nationalism in Wales with its parallels among the Basque, the Breton, the Quebecois and other ethnic minority groups in the developed world which he sees as failed nation states. In the post-war period the developed countries have produced an economy which is dependent on a new knowledge class – a group of technicians, administrators and managers – which lacks the financial power of the former elites but is a dominant and self-assertive force in modern society. The Welsh-speaking middle class is particularly interesting in this context. Virtually all are from working-class or lower middle-class homes in the mining villages and small towns of Wales, and are, therefore, without the inherited wealth and the public school experience of their counterparts in England. To this group ethnicity is a powerful sign of group identity and is being consciously utilized as a source of social power – most obviously through the school system.

The bilingual schools

According to the 1971 census, 20.8 per cent of the population in Wales can speak Welsh, but this fifth of the population are not spread evenly throughout the country. The density varies from 75.1 per cent in the most Welsh county to 2.1 per cent in the most anglicized county. The number of Welsh speakers continues to decline steadily: the Gittins Report (1968) estimates that 16 per cent of the children in Welsh primary schools were Welsh-speaking and the most recent survey from Welsh Education Office (1977) suggests a much lower figure.

The decline of the language is regarded with immense dismay by many Welshmen, and it was in an effort to protect the interests of Welsh speakers in anglicized areas that the first bilingual primary schools were opened in the 1950s. In these areas the old view, that the schools would teach English while the home and the community would look after Welsh, was no longer appropriate. In this instance the schools were regarded as successful in maintaining the language – a success which led in 1956 to the opening of Ysgol Glan Clwyd in Rhyl as the first bilingual secondary school. Now removed to Llanelwy, Ysgol Glan Clwyd has grown from an original 96 pupils to around 1200. In the last five years the bilingual school movement has grown and in 1978 there were 11 officially designated bilingual secondary schools mostly in the anglicized areas of south and east Wales but also in Bangor and Aberystwyth. The opening of bilingual schools in these university towns is no accident – with the introduction of a fully comprehensive system the bilingual schools have come to provide the only alternative secondary education, and to a growing number of middle-class parents it seems a better alternative.

The first bilingual schools were faced with a problem. In order to be accepted, and to win pupils in the face of competition from the established and highly respected grammar schools, they had to compete with these schools on their own terms. In other words, they had to prove themselves the equal in academic achievements to the grammar schools. In this they have been remarkably successful. Comparable figures are hard to obtain (they are not published) but Monks' (1968) research showed that one school with 100 per cent Welsh-speaking pupils had impressively high attainments. There is little else that can be got out of Monks' research, for the sample of seven Welsh schools compared with a number of English schools apparently includes only one officially designated bilingual school. Even so, the overall performance of the sample of schools in Wales was not significantly different from that of the English schools. But it is not only because of their academic achievements that the schools are regarded as superior. It is widely believed that discipline is better and morale higher in the bilingual schools than in the English schools. There is some evidence that this belief is based on a shrewd understanding of reality. Baum (1978) reports that attendance at an English-medium school was only 88.3 per cent compared with 93.5 per cent at a nearby bilingual school. He writes: 'The latter school is somewhat smaller, but in view of the identical catchment areas, it is difficult to dismiss the contrasting linguistic and cultural backgrounds of the pupils as a significant contributing factor to the difference.' Not only difficult, we may think, but wrong.

The pressure for Welsh-medium schools comes from a particular section of Welsh society and is often in opposition to the Welsh Education Office whose attitude to the schools is ambivalent. Several times it has refused LEAs permission to open bilingual secondary schools with fewer than 500 pupils, although there are several English-medium comprehensive schools of this size, and far smaller, in Wales. The recent rise in the number of bilingual schools, from six in 1973 to eleven in 1978, has been achieved with grudging consent from the Welsh Education Office.

The use of Welsh has declined sharply this century but it is quite impossible to establish the extent to which the decline has been hastened, or latterly hindered, by educational policies and school practices. Lewes (1977) sees the language decline as being primarily affected by the immigration of English-speaking monoglots – as in the South Wales coalfields. Past a certain critical point (which may vary according to historical circumstances), speakers of the minority language cease to use the language outside their homes (and sometimes even within them). Moreover, the language is not transmitted in homes that have become linguistically mixed through marriage. Language collapse can follow in a relatively short time – as happened to Welsh in the Wirral, the Forest of Dean and the greater part of Radnorshire where the language seems to have disappeared in a single generation. Schools in Wales were first asked to destroy the language; then to adopt it as a useful medium of instruction in the mastery of English; finally to help maintain, and even reinstate, the language in anglicized areas. There is no satisfactory evidence to show that any of these policies have been a major success. It seems likely, although the data is hard to interpret, that during the long period 1850–1910 the schools helped slowly to reduce the number of monoglot speakers and make Wales a bilingual nation. But many other factors, in particular, the in-migration of substantial numbers of English monoglot workers and the spread of English newspapers and books, also had an important impact and in some areas were obviously crucial. From 1910 onwards the English-medium grammar schools gave an additional impetus to the identification of Welsh with low status and delayed the emergence of an educated Welsh-speaking middle class. In any event, by 1950 only a relatively small number of elderly people were unable to speak English. It is most probable that the education system did contribute to the decline of the language, but it is misleading and unhelpful to examine individual social institutions without reference to the overall context. It will be argued in chapter 9 that the depth of the economic depression in Wales followed from its status as a primary producer; the country failed to develop a modern diversified industrial sector until during and after the Second World War, and, as a result of having gained control at local level, but not, of course, at national level, the political leadership used the educational system (the only effective tool they had) as a means of providing individual, if not community, development. Given all this, the schools could have done little else, and it is necessary to grasp the historical relationships in their entirety rather than hope to analyse the effects of one of these factors in a complex relationship. For the same reasons it is impossible to foretell the impact of the Welsh-medium schools: though we can understand how they came into being, to understand their success we must first consider how embedded they are in the social and economic structure of modern Wales.

Gaelic in Scotland

The parallels between the recent history of the Welsh language and the other indigenous minority language in Britain – Gaelic – are worth making for they emphasize the difficulty of constructing theories of language change and maintenance which are not rooted in particular historical conditions.

Durkacz (1977) shows that the 1872 Education Act (Scotland) killed Gaelic-medium education before it had really started. Even supporters of the Gaelic cultural revival movement saw no alternative to the integration of Gaeldom with mainstream English society. They were not concerned to preserve the language through the school system and did not oppose English-medium education. The most useful work of the current status of Gaelic is now MacKinnon's (1977) study of the Isle of Harris from which the following account draws extensively.

By the 1950s Gaelic was at a particularly low point. Ignored by wider society it was spoken only by the island crofters on Harris and Lewis and by small groups in isolated mainland pockets. The BBC broadcast only 90 minutes a week in Gaelic and there were few publications. No Gaelic was taught in the schools or in the universities, except as an archaic language of historical interest. According to the 1971 census, there are just under 89,000 Gaelic speakers with the greatest concentration, more than 80 per cent, in the Western Isles. In Harris, the decline of the population from 5,449 in 1911 to 2,879 in 1971 indicates the extent of depopulation in the remoter parts of the British Isles. Inevitably the age structure is unbalanced and ageing. The economy has been left underdeveloped, and unemployment in the early 1970s was 27 per cent – the highest in

Britain. The decline has been so severe that, during the 1930s, fishing in one of the off-islands ceased economic activity when there were no longer enough able-bodied men to pull the boats in and no money to buy a power winch. The island – a sizeable piece of land about three miles across – is now deserted. In Harris, crofting is the main employment, but the crofts do not provide an adequate income for a family, and most crofters supplement their income, wherever possible, by some other work: there is some weaving and fishing, but most of the extra money now comes from tourism. As usual this has been found a mixed blessing, and MacKinnon shows how the former north-south links between the islands have been severed by the new tourist-oriented ferries working between the islands' chief harbours and the nearest mainland port.

Gaelic is used only in the home between friends and neighbours and not at all in shops and offices. MacKinnon describes how waitresses in an island cafe, who talked and joked between themselves in Gaelic behind the open kitchen door, were embarrassed when MacKinnon addressed them in Gaelic and replied to him only in English. English incomers have been elected to the community councils and appointed to the various local and government organizations which have responsibility for the Highland and Islands. Only in the Presbyterian Church is Gaelic used in a community setting. MacKinnon argues that the Western Isles community has suffered a great blow by economic neglect and relates the high level of depressive illness and alcoholism to the near collapse of the indigenous culture.

In the last few decades there has been an improved recognition of Gaelic in the schools. The Gaelic Books Council was formed in 1969, and schools' broadcasting was introduced in 1970. But the low level of institutional support for Gaelic is indicated by MacKinnon's observation that, in 1972, there were no Gaelic books in the Harris public library. Although there is enthusiasm for the language amongst a number of teachers in Lewis and Harris, there is no responsibility on the LEA to appoint Gaelic-speaking staff even in the most Gaelic districts. MacKinnon also comments on the harm that has been caused by the closure of many small rural schools where the language is less strong. He writes: 'Centralization of educational facilities

97

clearly is to the detriment of Gaelic language-maintenance and its usage amongst schoolchildren. The presence of English monoglot children reinforces other social pressures and almost invariably results in the switch to English.' MacKinnon's survey of language usage showed that language loyalty was weakest among the high professional class but that there was evidence to show that the non-crofting working class had also begun to shift to English. In Harris, about 12 to 18 per cent of the primary age pupils were being brought up in English by Gaelic-speaking parents – a proportion which is certainly higher than that observed a decade ago. Mixed marriages also present a problem for the transmission of Gaelic, and only a very few English children learn the language. Overall, 86.6 per cent heard Gaelic at home, compared with 91.8 per cent in a 1957–8 survey.

There are no Gaelic high schools to match the Ysgolion Cymraeg and no Gaelic-medium instruction. The recent opening of Sabhal Mor Ostaing (the Gaelic college in Skye) and its emergence as a cultural centre for the whole island community is the one promising development. The case of Harris is particularly interesting because, although there is no significant degree of in-migration or economic development, there is, nevertheless, a language shift taking place. It seems particularly ironic that the highest degree of language loyalty amongst schoolchildren is with the boys and girls of the highest academic ability and lowest amongst the girls with the lowest academic abilities. As MacKinnon notes, it is the former who will leave the community and the latter who will stay and bring up their children, most probably, in English.

Summary and conclusion

Indigenous minorities in the rural areas have largely been overlooked as an area of concern both by policy makers and social scientists. This chapter has discussed educational provision for the Welsh and the Scottish Gaels. The Welsh now have a nearly adequate Welsh-medium primary school provision and a rapidly increasing bilingual secondary school provision. The Gaels have no Gaelic-medium schools and what little Gaelic teaching exists is at the mercy of administrators who have no statutory duty to provide it.

MacKinnon discusses four possible modes of language shift: clearance – where the indigenous people are forced to move out of the area; economic development – which argues that languages of technology and modernization (in this case English) replace unadapted folk languages (in this case Gaelic); changeover – in which minority language speakers adopt the language of an incoming minority group; and social morale – which supposes that an established community will lose confidence in it social values when confronted by an in-migrant group with superior economic and social power. MacKinnon believes that all of these have, to a varying extent, been operative in Scottish Gaeldom.

These ideas can be related to Wirth's conceptualization cited earlier. The first case, flight, is less a means of relating to a majority culture than a means of avoiding it and, although of transparent historical significance in explaining why these groups happen to be where they are, is of no current interest to those whose concern is with social relationships. The argument that languages which are the medium of a superior technology will displace a 'folk' language, although at one level obvious, does nothing to explain why that technology should be desired or adopted in the first instance. Again, to say that a community which has lost an historical struggle against a more powerful group of incomers will be demoralized and lose confidence in its own social values may be initially true. This was true of the Native Americans, it was true of the Maoris, but it was never completely true of the Welsh. Nor is it true for ever. Within a couple of generations, part of the incomers' culture is assimilated, part is rejected and new modes of adaptation to the new culture emerge.

In Wirth's terms the choice is between assimilation, pluralism, secession and militancy. The latter two have never been a real possibility for the groups discussed here; the idea of secession has attracted a number of Welsh writers and politicians but for the foreseeable future, at least, it looks a distinctly unlikely event. It is even less of a possibility for the other groups. Historically, the Celtic minorities have adopted an assimilationist policy. It has been shown how the Welsh used their control of the educational system to slowly direct this policy, which had originally been forced upon them by the central authorities in England, towards pluralism. The Gaels never gained local political control of the school system or of any of the other major institutions of the dominant society; in their case a policy of assimilation continued to be the only seemingly realistic choice. MacKinnon suggests that the effects of this are now, at last, working through into the family where the language is not being transmitted by parents who have adopted the assimilationist view. It is important to realize that the minority had little choice in the way they responded to the pressures from their powerful neighbours. The institutions of the dominant group are intended to condition how the institutions of the minority group adapt.

The post-war rise of Welsh national consciousness and its relations to the emergence of a sizeable Welsh-speaking middle class has been extensively discussed. The bilingual schools provide ironic verification of Barth's concept of resource competition, in that they are now perceived as a superior resource, the allocation of which is entirely reserved for Welsh speakers. This has created protest from non-Welsh speakers, who have no choice of schooling, and a marked rise in the number of Welsh learners in the catchment areas of the Welsh-speaking schools.

That the Gaels have been so unsuccessful, in comparison with the Welsh, in gaining recognition for their language in the school system may be related to the fact that they are twice removed from the centre of power. Although the Scottish educational system is independent, political decisions are made in England, and it is in England – in the national centre – that the Gaelic speakers would have had to make their claims.

To identify and analyse the relationships between the factors influencing language maintenance and ethnic consciousness within a body of formal theory, may be an unhelpful and impossible task. It may be that we have to settle for historically-situated discussion of individual cases which can then be compared along certain dimensions. It is even less likely that the impact of one social institution – the school – can be separated out. Nevertheless, a few points do seem clear and it might be worth listing them. It seems that schools can aid the development of bilingualism in a minority population, but the teaching of a minority language to the majority, as the lack of success with Irish suggests, is likely to fail unless, as in the Israeli case, there are strong political, economic or ideological reasons for not failing. Education through the majority language for minority speakers does seem to create one of the conditions necessary for out-migration. Finally, bilingual schools may be of some help in maintaining the language in mixed language homes by providing institutional support for the minority language partner and an additional setting for the use of the language by the child.

7

Support systems for rural education

In the developed world, the problems of rural education are essentially ones of ensuring that people living in remote and sparsely populated areas have the same access to education as those living in towns and cities. Sher (1977), chief consultant to the current OECD project Education in Sparsely Populated Areas, describes the basic problems of rural education as being:

1 The lack of access to generalized resources and services;
2 Diseconomies of scale, and
3 The lack of supporting institutions.

The eventual report will provide a wealth of information on the provision of education in the rural areas of England, France, New Zealand, Norway, Portugal, Scotland, Sweden, Switzerland and Western Australia.

This chapter will discuss the recent attempts to strengthen existing institutions and provide new support systems for rural education in three areas – Britain, Scandinavia and Australia and New Zealand. In Britain, a new concern with the problems of teaching in rural schools is reflected in teacher education and in the use of the teachers' centres to improve communication between widely scattered groups of village school teachers. Interest in community education in rural areas has waned since the days of the village colleges, and some of the recent initiatives are not based on the school system at all. The Western Islands Community Education project is one such scheme. In Scandinavia, there are some influential projects, reflecting significant policy changes, which deserve to be more widely known outside those countries. Teaching by correspondence was mentioned in chapter 5 as a useful addition to conventional teaching methods. At school level, the countries with the most experience of correspondence teaching are Australia and New Zealand, and since almost nothing is known of their practice to those not directly involved, it is worth giving a reasonably full account.

Initiatives in Britain

The James Report (1972) made a strong case against overdependence upon initial training and re-emphasized the importance of continuing teacher education. In-service education is the responsibility of no single body. In many LEAs it is an essential part of the advisory staffs' job to promote in-service training at different levels. The most common forms of in-service training are the short courses arranged in collaboration with a local college of education; others are supported by the DES and can be teacher-directed. These courses do not lead to formal qualifications but are recognized as signs of interest in gaining further skills and knowledge. The LEAs work closely with the colleges of education in providing in-service B Ed courses (Clwyd's scheme for rural teachers is a good example) and with the University Institutes of Education in providing M Ed courses. These can be studied full-time but are more usually taken over a period of years. The teachers' centres play a varied role: in some areas they are well integrated with in-service facilities whereas in others they are regarded exclusively as meeting places for teachers where LEA officials are not always welcome.

The essential problem for rural teachers is that of distance. It is very unlikely that a teacher will be willing to go out on a wintery evening, on a round trip of twenty or thirty miles on country lanes, to attend an in-service course, particularly as he might not be able to recover his travelling expenses. The solution adopted in some areas of Norway, to use blocks of time for in-service work, might be worth considering elsewhere.

There are few courses which deal specifically with the problems of teachers in small or remote schools. Some colleges have begun to recognize the particular need for a training course which would familiarize students with the particular problems of small rural primary schools. Bishop Grosseteste College of Education in Lincoln and Keswick Hall College of Education in Norwich have been pioneers in this field. At secondary level even less has been done, but there are some suggestions that experiments with the interchange of teachers might be worthwhile.

The role of the teachers' centres in formal, in-service education is often minimized by political considerations, but there are several teacher centre based initiatives in this field and one, mentioned briefly in chapter 4, is worth describing further. The small market town of Wigton, Cumbria, serves a wide area of upland farmsteads and small villages. The teachers' centre is on the third floor of an old primary school. Its main room holds twenty-five people in comfort and another ten at a pinch. There is a warden's office, a stock of books and records, film and slide projectors, tape recorders, cameras and other photographic equipment, stage lights, a duplicator, some maths and science apparatus, and facilities for making tea and coffee. The centre is staffed by a full-time warden, a supply head (when he's not on call) and two other supply teachers working half-time. There are four secondary schools and thirty-four primary schools, most of them two- and three-teacher schools serving the small villages around Wigton. Since the centre opened six years ago, the warden – Valerie Lerew – has concentrated her efforts on the needs of teachers working in these small and remote primary schools. She describes them as: '. . . a rather static, though conscientious, educational community, in which basic educational principles tend to get overwhelmed by the day-to-day problems, instead of providing a thread of strength and continuity from which to create a pattern which will attack and absorb those problems.' The warden sees her job as being to establish that life thread: to strengthen teachers' confidence in their own abilities and to encourage innovation. As part of this programme she has built up a resource bank of teachers whose specialist skills can be called upon, established strong personal links between the team, the schools and the LEA advisory service and has tried to provide teachers with a framework of resources which can enable them to develop their own curriculum changes. A start has been made on encouraging groups of schools to work together (not only in sports), and it is hoped to have a strategically placed mini-bus to make this possible. Teachers working from the centre have already developed several curriculum projects, the most challenging perhaps being an environmental studies scheme in which a number of small schools have co-operated with the local radio station to produce a series of programmes which can be used by other schools in the locality and, indeed, over a much wider area. The warden comments:

> I would like to see develop a much greater emphasis on local and personal resources. Over the last few years we have, both socially and educationally, been conditioned to think that money and materials, equipment and posh furniture, are the answer to all ills and that without them we cannot function. Hence teachers saying we cannot do this because we have not got that.

The point is worth emphasizing. The first people to believe that improved facilities and more materials necessarily mean better education are the teachers themselves. In the small schools – with low purchasing power – this can become a demoralizing and self-fulfilling doctrine.

The ratio of rhetoric to action in community education is probably higher than in any other area of the subject. MacLeod's (1977) account of the Western Islands Community Education Project is not only refreshingly free of grandiose statements of aims but is also worth discussing because it relates back to MacKinnon's studies of a similar community, mentioned in chapter 6, and adds a useful perspective to the picture presented there.

105

The remote Western Islands of Scotland have been relatively little affected by modernization. The economy is still based on crofting and in-shore fishing, and the people are still predominantly Gaelic speaking. There are fifteen secondary schools on the islands, mostly situated in the small towns. Because of the relative underdevelopment of the area, there is considerable out-migration by the most educated young people. All secondary education is through the medium of English, and it is only in recent years that some Gaelic has been introduced into the primary schools. The Community Education Project, funded in part by charitable foundations and in part by government agencies, was established in 1975 with the aim of strengthening community organizations at all levels. The focus has been on pre-school education and youth work. In the district where most of the effort has been concentrated, a thriving pre-school playgroup has been formed with the enthusiastic help of the mothers. The meetings are held in Gaelic, and a number of books and tape recordings of stories and rhymes in Gaelic have been produced in collaboration with a special bilingual education project. The youth group has also been successful and has been engaged in local community service projects. At another level, farmers and crofters have shown interest in the formation of purchasing and marketing co-operatives of the kind that have been so beneficial to similar communities in the west of Ireland. The project workers see their task as being to stimulate interest and to leave the organizations in the hands of the people themselves, once they have acquired the necessary skills in management and fund raising. MacLeod comments that most villages have fine new halls which are scarcely used because of lack of knowledge about how to initiate the sorts of organizations which would be helpful. The project is still in progress, and it is too soon to assess its impact on the communities, but the interim reports are encouraging.

Developments in Scandinavia

The population in the northern areas of Norway has been declining at an increasing rate in recent years, to such an extent that the continued existence of once thriving communities is now

106

seriously in doubt. An OECD report (1976) gives the population of North Norway as 464,000 with a low density of about 4.5 persons per square kilometre, but out-migration during the period 1961–71 averaged 3,300 a year. There are, however, recent indications that the depopulation trend may be reversing but, without long-term regional development, the situation is not promising. The Norwegian government is anxious to halt, and if possible, reverse this decline for two reasons. First, without relatively strong balanced communities in the remote areas, the important resources on land and at sea would be underexploited. It is less expensive in the long run, and preferable on other grounds also, to maintain a balanced community which can have an important supporting role in the servicing of essential workers in the fishing, forestry and oil industries rather than have to support, from distant urban centres, the marketing, communications, administration and medical needs of both the residual ageing population of a declining township and the nucleus of essential workers. Second, the position of Norway makes it vitally important to the defensive strategy of the NATO powers, and any serious weakening of its population base in the northern areas increases its vulnerability. The problem of depopulation caused by urban drift is, consequently, taken seriously in Norway, and the educational system has been heavily criticized for the, albeit unintended, contribution it has made by providing young people with the opportunities for out-migration.

Much of the recent educational legislation in Norway has been prompted by a desire to harmonize educational opportunities in urban and rural districts. It was a matter of concern that the proportion of rural children entering the gymnasium (grammar school equivalent) was much lower than the proportion in urban areas.

Lindbekk (1969) shows that the percentage of children entering realskole (14–16 years) varied from 80 per cent, in some geographical regions, to zero in others. The percentage was lowest in the peripheral centres where out-migration was highest. Working-class entry was considerably influenced by the distance of the nearest school – even a short journey of ten kilometres was enough to noticeably lower the percentage of

107

working-class children entering the realskole. When a fully comprehensive school system was introduced in the 1960s, it was considered necessary to create large centralized schools which involved rural children in travelling very considerable distances. The motives behind this reorganization were clearly to provide equal opportunities for all children and to ensure that all available talent was being utilized in the interests of national efficiency. But, in effect, it led to the importation of a school culture out of sympathy with the economic foundations and traditions of the rural communities. The educational system directed young people away from their own communities by teaching values which were at variance with those of the community and its own needs. It defined the important knowledge as being that suitable for occupations outside the community.

During the period 1969–72 several surveys were made of the effects of school centralization, following heavy criticism of the policy, concerning such matters as teacher recruitment, effects of transport, educational achievements in large and small schools and so on. A major research study by Solstad (1975), carried out in fifty-four schools throughout Norway concluded:

> There seem to be no systematic differences between types of school defined by degree of centralization and size, either as regards general abilities or motive [attitude to school]. Furthermore, no pattern emerged that indicates a clear relationship between type of settlement in the catchment area (for instance urban–rural) on the one hand and ability level or motive strength on the other.

For example, in the ninth grade (16 years) the average score, on a measure of attitude to school, was 5.37 in small schools with a low degree of centralization (less than 50 per cent bussed in) and 4.92 in large schools with a high degree of centralization (more than 50 per cent bussed in). The amount of time spent on homework was 86.6 minutes, compared with 76.4 minutes per day respectively. To put the matter plainly, small schools with a low degree of centralization proved significantly better on both measures. The research also found that children who had to travel long distances to school were in poorer physical condition than those who travelled shorter distances or walked.

In response to the high level of concern with the negative aspects of the centralization policy and the non-local bias of the curriculum, a project was established to work with teachers in the remote Lofoten Islands. These islands are dependent on seasonal cod fishing from January to April, and the introduction of compulsory secondary education in 1969 was felt to seriously interfere with the cod industry, and particularly threatened the career patterns of the boys. Instead of being able to learn the main business of the community first hand, they were in school learning knowledge that would only be useful to them elsewhere. The project involves the seven youth schools in Lofoten in the production of a locally-based social studies syllabus including the use of textbooks, a teachers manual, slide series and tape recordings. These materials are used as the basis for students' project work and replace the former nationally-based course. Høgms and Solstad (1977), the project directors, believe that the attitude that rural life must be compared with urban life in terms of the facilities available must be opposed as false, and that the aim of planners and educationists should be to regard the community as a foundation of common experience. In this context it is vital that every community should have its own school:

> A school that does not ignore problems that are relevant to the people it serves, that stresses the relations between the local area and units at regional and national level, that shows how the local dialect has its grammatical rules and special concepts, and that its own community has a history and tradition in the same way as any other group of people, may enable its children to develop the feeling of being members of a fully respected community. This is probably in most cases a precondition for developing the amount of self-confidence that is necessary for entering into co-operative work as equal partners or to risk new approaches to problems.

The introduction of the new scheme has met a certain amount of resistance from some parents and teachers and has not been universally adopted. Nevertheless, it represents a distinct change in attitude towards the remoter settlements and proposes a profound change in the function of education from one which provides for social mobility to one which helps to integrate students into the community and thus helps strengthen it. The experiment is still underway and it is too early to reach any conclusions about its success either in the narrower aim of providing integrated locally-based studies relevant to the children of the community, or in its much wider aim of helping to stem the outward migration of potentially valuable members of the community. No one supposes that education in itself can achieve this but in co-operation with other planning agencies the hope is that a real change in the function of the educational system can be achieved.

Special emphasis has been given in Norway to the provision of in-service education and information resources. Stolen (1975) describes the sparsely populated district of More and Romsdal which has 228 primary schools (27 per cent one-teacher or two-teacher schools) 42 small combined primary/secondary schools and 30 comprehensive schools in addition to the vocation schools and six folk high schools. In order to deal with the problem of keeping the 2,200 teachers in touch with changing developments in education, which were becoming increasingly great, the school authority decided to reduce the school year by one week and to provide forty hours paid leave which teachers could take at any convenient occasions during the school year. These periods are spent in refresher courses, attending lectures on new teaching methods, working on joint projects and so on. Experience is showing that the new scheme is popular and achieving its aims.

The village colleges discussed in chapter 2 were influenced, perhaps to a greater extent than Henry Morris liked to admit, by the successful folk high schools first established in Denmark. They developed, of course, from an entirely different set of conditions. Paulston (1974) shows that throughout Scandinavia the folk high school has been an important educational and social force for more than a century. During the mid-nineteenth century education in Denmark, where the folk high schools originated, was controlled by the Church and the State and it was illegal (as it was in England and Wales) for elementary schools to provide any form of secondary education. The mass of the peasant farmers received only a minimum level of schooling and for the few who went on to secondary school the traditional Latin curriculum offered only the possibility of individual advancement. The folk high schools were started in the mid-nineteenth century by a leading churchman Bishop Grundvig, whose much quoted statement: 'Dead are all letters even if written by the fingers of Angels, and dead is all knowledge which does not find response in the life of the reader', expresses his fundamental attitude. The folk high schools were financed and run by their local communities and offered post-elementary education to boys and girls aged eighteen and over. The usual pattern was a winter course of five months for men and a summer course of three months for women. The courses were practically based and of special relevance to the needs of the farming community.

In the 1880s when the world agricultural depression hit Danish farmers they responded to American competition by switching from grain production to intensive dairy and bacon farming and by developing co-operative purchasing and marketing organizations. The Danish folk high schools were extremely important in assisting this development and were intimately involved with the radical movement which finally led to the defeat of the landowning class at the turn of the twentieth century.

The success of the folk high schools in providing further education under popular control led to their adoption in neighbouring countries and there are now about 100 in Sweden, 75 in Norway and 85 in Finland. Their original function of providing post-elementary education is no longer so important with universal secondary education but it is estimated that some 10 per cent of the 20-year age group attend for courses in literature, language, and practical subjects. In addition to the youth courses it has become a popular way to spend a holiday and family groups enrol for two-week summer courses in a variety of subjects. The schools are still independent of government control although most of the running costs are met by government funds and there are grants available for those unable to afford the fees.

Distance teaching in Australia and New Zealand

Among economically developed countries Australia is perhaps the most sparsely populated area in the world. New Zealand, too, is overwhelmingly rural. In New Zealand it has always been considered essential to provide education for the farming community and the 1877 Education Act took particular note of the needs of the rural population. In 1900 two-thirds of New Zealand's population lived on farms or in small settlements and 80 per cent of primary schools were one- or two-teacher units. Like all developed countries the New Zealand towns and cities have grown at the expense of the countryside and by 1966 only 23 per cent of the school population lived in the rural areas and over the years extensive consolidation of rural schools has taken place. However, each of New Zealand's main islands is the size of England with a total population of barely 3 million: the population of the North Island is $2\frac{1}{2}$ million with well over a third living in Auckland and Wellington; the population of the South Island is only 500,000 with large concentrations in Christchurch and Dunedin. It is clear that huge areas of New Zealand are very thinly populated and for children living in such areas who cannot get to a local school the correspondence school provides the alternative.

The New Zealand Correspondence School was founded in 1922 to provide education for children in remote areas. It might have been expected that with improved transport facilities the need for the school would have declined but the reverse has happened: between 1940 and 1970 the enrolment had more than doubled to reach 7,000 and by 1977 had almost doubled again. There are now about 12,750 students. The number of full-time school-age pupils include 690 in the primary section, 668 in the secondary section, 297 seriously handicapped children following a home training programme, and 196 in need of special (mainly remedial) courses. A further 1,526 pupils enrolled at other schools also receive correspondence school lessons in one or more subjects. The school began an experimental pre-school education course in 1976 and now has more than 300 under-fives enrolled. The bulk of the school's work is now with adults: of these, part-time adult students – mostly studying to complete

School Certificate – make up half the total enrolment; the remainder are teachers, more than 2,000, the majority studying for advanced or specialized qualifications, others following refresher courses after a period of teaching, and a small number of uncertificated teachers finishing their initial training. With 269 teachers and numerous administrative staff the correspondence school is easily the largest school in New Zealand.

The basic teaching device is the printed assignment, prepared by the correspondence school staff, containing sufficient material for two weeks work. These are supplemented by radio broadcasts; tape cassettes for music, languages and, increasingly, for personal contact between teacher and pupil; three-dimensional materials including practical kits; additional visual aids, and, of course, textbooks. Great efforts are made to ensure that pupils are able to meet their teacher and each other during the course of the year. Five district teachers aim to make a home visit to each pupil at least once a year and other visiting teachers are able to provide specialist tuition where necessary. The month-long residential summer course provides the main opportunity for pupils and their teachers to get to know each other and, in addition, there are frequent weekend seminars, especially for older pupils, and parents are encouraged to attend the annual Parents' Association Conference in Wellington with their children. A recently introduced telephone contact service intended for emergencies has also proved useful.

Most of the school's full-time pupils study at home where they are supervised by their mothers. According to a correspondence school survey by McVeagh (1977) more than half of the mothers managed to supervise their children for between 20–9 hours each week and, although nearly a quarter said they had considerable difficulty in settling the children down to work, only a small minority of mothers were able to give their children less than 10 hours supervision. In addition to the home-based students there are a number of pupils in small remote primary schools in the charge of an uncertificated teacher who are able to benefit from dual enrolment. These pupils follow the basic correspondence school programme, and have the opportunity of attending the summer school and the other group activities of the correspondence school, but are supervised outside the home and gain from their daily involvement together. Correspondence school courses have proved to be so popular with other secondary schools that severe restraint has been placed upon their use; headteachers who wish to enrol pupils with the correspondence school must first obtain permission from the district senior inspector. The most popular subjects are Maori, French, technical drawing and mathematics in forms three and four, studied by 31 per cent of the students; technical drawing, mathematics, commercial practice and biology in form five, studied by 34 per cent of the students; and economics, accounting, music, physics, technical drawing and Maori in forms six and seven, studied by 25 per cent of the students. This is seen as a special service intended to help schools over a temporary staffing difficulty, to provide opportunities for students who wish to enter a particular occupation, or (in the case of Maori) to provide appropriate cultural education.

It is difficult to obtain worthwhile information about the effectiveness of the correspondence school in comparison with other schools. The available figures suggest that at School Certificate level home-based, full-time, school-age pupils do slightly worse than the average for other rural schools. However, students enrolled while attending other schools do slightly better. More than half of the full-time pupils were enrolled late and many were enrolled precisely because they were ill or experiencing other problems (for example, pregnancy) which were interfering with their studies. In view of this it is generally accepted that the correspondence school is at least as effective as conventional schooling. It is also cheaper; the average per capita cost for primary school pupils is $350 per annum compared with $275 for pupils in the correspondence school. A lower, but still substantial, differential exists between the secondary school costs.

In Australia, the first School of the Air opened in 1951 at Alice Springs. There are now twelve schools able to use the Flying Doctor two-way radio communication channel which enables a class of pupils scattered over thousands of square miles of bush to take part in assemblies, drama and other joint activities. The number of pupils served by these schools is declining as fewer people live in the outback and as increasing prosperity enables pupils to be bussed fifty or sixty miles each way daily to attend school in the town, but, to very remote pupils, they are still important. Starr (1978) describes the school at Port Augusta, South Australia, with five teachers and 80–90 pupils some living over 700 kilometres away. In this school each teacher has responsibility for the preparation and marking of lessons for about fifteen pupils. These are formed into groups of two to eight pupils each with a daily call-in time for twenty minutes two-way communication. Larger groups are formed for social studies and art. Tutorial sessions with individual pupils permit the teacher to build up personal relationships and are seen as crucially important.

Summary and conclusion

In recent years there has been a new concern with the problem of education in the sparsely populated areas of the developed countries. In Norway, this can be seen as a response to the economic and strategic importance of the northern regions where depopulation has weakened the social fabric of many communities. The reforms of the 1960s – consolidated schools and a non-local curriculum – which were introduced without research have proved to be unnecessary or actually harmful. The special needs of rural areas are now being recognized in teacher training and by in-service programmes. Community education in rural areas has a long history; the development of the Danish folk high schools and the Cambridgeshire village colleges makes an interesting comparison. It may seem that the Scandinavian model has been more successful. In New Zealand, correspondence education has been especially well developed for children who cannot easily get to a local school and in Australia – where the word 'remote' has a dimension of meaning unknown to Europeans – the Schools of the Air provide a unique educational experience for children living in the outback. Both might have something to offer to other countries.

8

Education in the less developed rural world

Since the end of the Second World War, and the development of the United Nations Organization, the poorer countries of the world have demanded recognition of their problems. The terms used to describe these poor countries are variously political and economic. The term 'third world' reflects their supposed non-aligned stance between the capitalist Western powers and the communist Eastern powers. The terms 'underdeveloped', 'developing' and 'less developed' refer to their economic status and, since some poor countries are not developing at all, are often euphemisms. The term 'less developed countries' (LDCs) is the current favourite and will be adopted here. In this category are included most of the countries of three continents: Latin America, Asia and Africa, containing some two-thirds of the total world population. The unstable terminology reflects the problems of defining what is meant by 'less developed'.

There are many measures of development; the standard indicator, per capita Gross National Product (GNP), can be criticized for underestimating the self-sufficient, non-market economy of poor countries and for overestimating much of the circular expenditure of developed economies, but it is still a reasonable indicator of rank differences, if not of exact differences. Other indicators include diet, clothing, housing, sanitation, health, energy, transport, percentage of urban population, levels of literacy and so on.

Not all LDCs are equally poor. For example, Latin American countries are generally richer than Asian and African countries. In some small states, where the absence of a huge rural population adds to their political stability, outside capital has stimulated remarkable growth; Singapore and Hong Kong are the obvious examples. Korea and Taiwan are also developing with outside capital. In addition to these so-called 'export platforms' revenues from oil have made several Middle Eastern states extremely wealthy and Iran, in particular, is, or was, rapidly industrializing. Venezuela and Nigeria also benefit from oil. The size of the problems that still have to be faced should not allow us to overlook the fact that in the non-communist LDCs, generally, output per head rose by 75 per cent in the period 1950–70. Although, as Lipton (1977) points out, this rise in living standards has largely been enjoyed by the urban minority and has not been shared, even in such basic indicators as food consumption, with the rural poor.

The process of underdevelopment

There are different views about how these countries came to be so much poorer than the now rich countries. The conventional view, put emphatically by Bauer (1976), is that these countries were simply left behind by the industrial revolution which changed Europe and have gained considerably from Western influences including colonialism. Others see history somewhat differently. Hoogvelt (1976) and Frank (1971) regard underdevelopment as a process.

At some point in the sixteenth century it is suggested that many areas of the now less developed world – particularly India and China – were at a similar stage of social and economic development to Europe. Europe moved ahead at this time in the crucial fields of shipbuilding (and navigation) and the development of firearms. With this superior technology the Europeans

117

were able to trade on favourable terms with the East. A reminder of the profitability of the long mercantalist period can be seen in the now perhaps faded splendour of the European cities, notably Amsterdam and Venice, which were built with the profits of this trade. During the next few centuries the Europeans dominated trading through powerful merchant companies. The policies of these companies profoundly affected the societies they traded with. In India the rule of the princes was consolidated and, with exceptions, the development of indigenous industries was suppressed; in Africa, the fearsome slave trade weakened the structure of society and prevented the development of central authority; in Latin America, the established societies were utterly defeated and colonial rule imposed; in China, autonomous political and economic growth was hindered by harsh conditions of trade supported, when deemed necessary, by armed intervention. In the second half of the nineteenth century those parts of the African continent which had not already been colonized were hastily divided up between the European powers. The colonies were developed for their essential primary products – minerals, cocoa, vegetable oils and so on. The exploitation of these was sometimes in the hands of settler farmers, as in Kenya, Tanganyika and Rhodesia, and in other places in the hands of native farmers who sold their produce to European marketing companies, as in Ghana and Nigeria. The aim of the colonial power was to make its colonies financially self-supporting through local taxation, which meant the introduction of wage labour, the production of cash crops and, in many areas, the importation of an alien trader class. After decolonization in the post-war period the financial relationship between the former colonies and the colonial powers has continued through the process of neo-colonialism. Most former colonies are still dependent on one or two primary products, which are still marketed by Western companies in the currency of the dominant trading partner.

This model of history is rejected by those who take little account of the long debilitating period of mercantalism and who regard the colonial experience as beneficial rather than harmful. Goldthorpe (1975), who takes this view, writes: '. . . exploitation under colonial rule did occur at some times and in some places, though not everywhere and at all times, and . . . generally speaking colonial rule became less exploitative as it went on.' To a great extent this is simply a matter of definitions reflecting prior ideological commitments. There is less dispute about the effect of colonialism and neo-colonialism, or economic dependency. First, the new states, particularly in Africa, typically have little relationship to natural boundaries, either of geography or ethnicity, and this is an obvious destabilizing factor in many states with clear implications for educational and language policy. Second, it has led to the development of a dual economy, a modernized urban-based sector of industrial development, cash crop agriculture, transport, communication and government apparatus, and an underdeveloped near subsistence rural economy.

Strategies for development

The discussion about the origin of the LDCs is by no means academic for the theories of development and underdevelopment and the practical policies which follow from them are intimately connected. The conventional theory is essentially a deficit model which sees the process of modernization as being to make the less developed countries more like the developed countries, i.e. highly industrialized, urbanized and with the mental attitudes thought to be appropriate. There are debates about the best means to achieve this goal. Some economists, for example Nurske (1970), prefer the balanced growth approach with broadly based industrial development and considerable emphasis on agriculture, while other economists, for example Hirschman (1958), propose concentrated development in so-called poles of growth – industrial and commercial centres which should serve to uplift the backward economy of the surrounding region. Still others, for example Dumont (1963), place far more emphasis on the need to develop agriculture. Both of the first strategies have been criticized for perpetuating the dual economy and creating massive strains in developing nations: over-urbanization, unemployment and sizeable differentials in living conditions for the urban elite and the rural poor. Dumont's forceful criticism of conventional growth

119

strategies has been influential in converting many western development experts and some African leaders – notably Nyerere – to the need for national development based on agriculture and intermediate technologies. Some writers, indeed, do not believe that the world can stand the drain on resources that would be caused by world-wide industrialization to the level of Europe, North America, Japan and Australasia. But this view is, naturally, unattractive to third world leaders and has, perhaps, been given insufficient serious attention by international development agencies.

Education and national development

Few indigenous schools developed in the LDCs. All societies had a traditional, village-based, informal education which prepared children for life in the local community. In Muslim areas the Koranic schools provided instruction in religion, reading and writing, but it was the nineteenth-century Christian missionaries who brought schools to most areas. The mission schools, and later the government schools, provided an education geared to the production of essential personnel: tax collectors, messengers, bookkeepers, clergy, teachers, interpreters, clerks and artisans for government service. In the immediate pre-independence period provision was commonly extended to university level for administrators and a limited number of lawyers, doctors and other higher professional workers. The education systems of the colonial countries were thus geared to the production of an urban elite. Only a very few children were able to go to secondary school, and those who did were given aspirations for urban life where a post in government service gave a regular, if not large, income and where the conveniences of water, electricity, medical and other services were available.

School-based education has been adopted almost everywhere as an institution of great power for change. The school serves many functions. First, it is regarded as a basic human right that all children should receive at least an elementary level of schooling. Children who are denied the opportunity to become literate are cut off from participation in national life and denied the possibility of personal development. Second, the school is a

120

powerful instrument of social control and is invariably used to transmit the ideology of the dominant social class, to inculcate attitudes of responsibility and loyalty to the state and so on. Third, it legitimates access to the elite groups through 'objective' certification. Fourth, it is believed to be causally related to economic development.

The extent to which the underdevelopment of typical third world economies is due to a shortage of skilled labour is problematic. Some economists, for example, Anderson and Bowman (1965) and Harbison (1973), regard investment in human capital through the production of a skilled labour force as the essential solution to the problems of underdevelopment. But the relationship between education and economic development is by no means apparent and, as Adams (1977) shows, many other economists, pointing to the high levels of unemployment among secondary school and university graduates in several LDCs, see shortage of resources and lack of financial capital as being far more important. The tendency for school pupils to migrate to the cities has been an embarrassment to many countries unable to provide employment for more than a minority of these young people, who constitute a large unemployed and underemployed group whose skills are lost to the rural areas where they might be valuable. It is for these reasons that developing countries, which spend up to one-third of their budget on education, are having second thoughts about the relationship between education and development and are taking a tighter control over educational provision, even to the extent as Foster (1977), who seems to approve of the strategy, notes, of making political statements about the need to expand education while, in fact, reducing its funds and stabilizing levels of intake. The relationship between school-learned skills and economic growth is complicated by so many factors that no directly causal relationship can be found. Nevertheless, there is an evident need for appropriately trained workers in the administrative and modern sector of the economy and the school has been accepted as the place where they should be trained. The manpower planning approach is that adopted by most LDCs, although most countries also find it necessary to take into account the level of social demand (a politically sensitive issue), the level of resources available and the real cost to the

121

economy of their diversion into educational expenditure.

There is some evidence that schooling does affect the attitudes of students. Inkeles and Smith (1974) report that a cluster of traits – openness to new ideas, independence from traditional authority, respect for science and medicine, level of ambition for self and children, consciousness of the need for punctuality and planning, an interest in politics and national affairs – correlate highly with level of education. Many other writers, for example Myrdal (1968) are convinced that the obstacles to modernization lie in the attitudes of the population. They believe that it is traditional attitudes, rather than lack of resources and capital to get them into production, which are primarily responsible for holding back the development of third world countries and see schooling as the crucial instrument in introducing modern attitudes conducive to economic development. Others, like Keddie (1973), reject the distinction between traditional and Western rationality as a false dichotomy erected by Western scientists whose normative theoretical stance causes them to regard other cultures as deficient in relation to their own. Even those who might accept this distinction are doubtful about the influence of education as a means of change, Goldthorpe (1975) reports the research of Ogionwo (1969), for example, who was unable to find any relationship between innovative farming in Nigeria and educational level.

The dominant perspective held by nearly everyone concerned – Western intellectuals (Illich (1972) excepted), the governments of the LDCs and their people – regards schooling as essentially a good thing.

Rural education

If the arguments that schooling needs to be provided are accepted, then the size of the problem is daunting. Phillips (1975) quotes UNESCO estimates (which exclude China and North Vietnam) from a 1972 base forecasting that 71 million children will have less than four years schooling by 1975. Some will never attend (either through lack of a school or through parental decision), others will withdraw before completing their course. In Africa and Asia the number of children out of school is likely to rise rather than fall in succeeding years as population growth in most countries in those continents now exceeds the growth in school enrolments. In addition to this purely quantitive dimension there is the matter of quality. Buildings are commonly sub-standard, teachers often poorly trained, textbooks and materials scarce and administration and inspection inefficient. Teaching is usually confined to the instruction of reading and arithmetic by oral drill. In answer to a UNESCO survey, carried out by Brimer and Pauli (1971), about half of the respondents stated that the school curriculum was inadequate for their specific local and national needs. Most of these deficiencies are linked to the shortage of money but it is not clear that this is the only, or even the essential, reason. Although several African states spend around 20–40 per cent of their revenue on education about a quarter of this (not equally distributed of course) comes from foreign aid. Moreover, the cost of maintaining a school at local level, however great the cost of the system may be nationally, is not cripplingly high for most local communities as the growth of the indigenous Kenyan Harambee schools indicates. Jolly (1971) writes: 'In Africa, shortage of finances is often *treated* as the constraint to further educational expansion particularly at primary level. Yet it is just at this level where persons with the education required to be primary teachers are unemployed.' He suggests that the educational movement in Cuba shows that educational provision is as much a matter of political will and commitment as of funds.

Rural education and development

The characteristic feature of the LDCs – those at least without strict control on population movement – is their rapid urbanization. Africa is the most obvious example. Thirty years ago there were only five towns south of the Sahara with more than 100,000 inhabitants; today there are 70. In Zaire, an extreme example, the change has been so great that 40 per cent of the population live in one town, Brazzaville. This is not an indication of economic prosperity but the very reverse; it is caused by the flight from the impoverished rural areas of people in search of increasingly hypothetical employment in the towns. Recently,

Foster (1975) and Lipton (1977), who see the main problems of the LDCs as resulting from urban bias, have argued that much of this urbanization is a statistical artefact resulting from expanding city boundaries and the conflation of internal city growth by migration patterns which, typically, are short-term and caused by factors of rural push (poverty and lack of employment) rather than urban pull (generally high level of services). In any case, whatever the overall trend, the less developed countries are predominantly rural – in India, Pakistan, Indonesia and in most African states some 80 per cent of the population earn their living on the land. It was mentioned above that education cannot be separated from the question of development and it has been accepted by many authorities that development must be based on agriculture, or at least must not disregard it, and that education must be brought to make a more positive contribution to the entire process. Among those now converted to this view is the Ministry of Overseas Development (1970) (now absorbed into the Foreign Office) whose report recommends non-academic courses of primary education, the equitable spread of resources to training young adults, and the concentration on community development as the most appropriate means of raising the living standards of the agricultural population, and regards the careful selection of aid as essential in supporting this policy.

The most powerful statement of this position comes from Malassis (1976). He argues that the less developed countries will not develop (like the West) through the transfer of resources from agriculture to industry. The equation is simple; an increase of 6 per cent in the economic growth rate, combined with a demographic increase of 3 per cent from a population base of 80 per cent rural and 20 per cent urban, implies an increase of 2.25 per cent a year in the rural population. Urban-based industrial development, which outstrips the rural sector, results in out-migration of the younger elements of the population most of whom will be unemployed or underemployed and a burden in the urban system at the very time when they might be contributing to rural development. The loss of these young people further weakens the rural economy sometimes to the point where it is no longer able to supply the urban population with food, as is now the case in more than one African country. Malassis puts a great deal of blame for this – more than is really justified perhaps – on the educational system.

The newly independent colonies made the Western concept of the educated man their ideal, and imported systems of education which divorce liberal education from technical education, and downgrade vocational and manual work. This system, which Bourdieu and Passeron (1977) show to have developed historically as a means of legitimating bourgeois cultural capital through certification, has been imported into a totally alien setting. It concentrates on full-time child education to the neglect of youth and adult education. Its academic curriculum neglects the process of development and ignores the analysis of the national problem. There are few observers unaware of the nature of the educational system in the LDCs. Lipton (1977) writes:

> In most poor countries today the process of rural education and its aftermath is a huge sieve, through which the ablest young people pass to the cities, there to help the urban elite. The content of rural schooling is largely irrelevant to rural needs; and, by being enabled to retain its intelligent young leaders for agricultural development, the *rural sector in almost every poor country would benefit from the termination of rural education*.

Despite his emphasis of the last point Lipton does not actually advocate this, but his pessimistic view of the system gives him no confidence in its potential development role. The educational system is poorly geared to the problem of socio-economic development, either in content or method, is ineffective as an agency of rural improvement, is extremely costly and incapable of generating radical change.

Malassis is well aware that the separate development of a 'rural education', which has long been recognized, for example by Foster (1965), as an error, would be a retrograde step. Attempts to introduce such schemes have failed in several countries because of parents' refusal to send their children to first schools which do not offer the possibility of advancement to secondary stage. The introduction of agriculture or related sub-

125

jects into the curriculum of the existing schools has been an even more dismal failure. In Nigeria, where agriculture was offered for some years at secondary school, the subject was dropped when it was revealed that only a handful of pupils had ever entered the examination. In Ghana, where rural science was taught, it was found that only 2 per cent of the students returned to farming. In all countries schools have come to be seen as the means by which access is gained to the urban elite whose life style contrasts favourably with that endured by the rural majority. Quite apart from this, there is seen to be little point in gaining an academic knowledge of modern farming practices when little, if any, of it could be applied to the local situation without capital and without continuing support from rural development agencies. In view of this Malassis proposes that educationists must cease to look at the school in isolation and without reference to its social context. The whole educational system must be linked to rural progress through conventional agricultural extension services but also through community development, or, in the French term, *animacion*, and through co-operation with other institutions to promote long term development based on the mass of the population. Only in this way can the rural people participate in the business of creating and sharing in economic growth and if they cannot, they will not stay.

Educational technology

Modern techniques of mass communication have made a marked impact on the LDCs. The transistor radio is a prized possession in the poorest villages of India, Africa and Latin America. It is hardly unsurprising that the potential of these media in the formal educational process should have been left unexplored. A great number of national and international agencies have been involved with studies of the potential or actual use of the new technology in the LDCs. The OECD Centre for Educational Research and Innovation (CERI) is particularly active and the former British Ministry of Overseas Development's Centre for Educational Television Overseas (CETO) and Centre for Curriculum Renewal and Educational Development

126

Overseas (CREDO) are more than euphonious acronyms. There are also several US agencies and others, like the South East Asian Innotech, which aim to improve the educational service through the application of media technology. It is, however, widely agreed that most of the schemes that have been implemented have either been unsuccessful – as in Niger – or owe their limited success to parallel work in teacher training and supervision – as in the case of El Salvador, Ivory Coast and American Samoa. At the present time the opinion of most independent observers (those not involved in sales, research and development) is that educational technology is too expensive, too liable to equipment failure (and the schools do not have the knowledge to repair breakdowns) and an unnecessary burden on LDCs, offering them nothing that could not be done better by a well-trained teacher with an adequate supply of basic equipment. At a less sophisticated level there are developments in the production of learning packages for science and the provision of correspondence courses which look useful, although MacDonald and Walker (1976) suggest that the experience of the Schools Council projects in Britain gives good reason to believe that centre disseminated innovations are invariably modified by teachers in practice and rarely have a marked or lasting effect in changing teaching methods.

Education in two African states

This discussion may be more easily comprehended by detailed reference to educational provision in particular countries. The following pages attempt to describe education in two African states which have adopted contrasting development strategies and consequently different educational policies.

Nigeria

Nigeria is the largest of the African states with a population of 80 million and a land area three times the size of Britain The land varies from hot rain forest, through warm grassland, to hot near desert in the north. Seven main ethnic groups make up four-fifths of the population but there are a great many smaller tribal groups. In the north, the people are mainly Muslim and there is a tradition of indigenous Koranic schools. In the south and west, Christianity is the common religion and the history of mission schools goes back more than a century. The Federation of Nigeria, created in 1960, gave the three major regions considerable autonomy but after the 1967–70 civil war the country was re-organized into twelve smaller states to reduce instability. Colonial and post-colonial development led to the growth of the coastal ports and Ibadan as industrial and commercial centres. The discovery of oil, in 1956, led to further rapid development in the west. The major economic divisions in Nigeria are thus between the relatively urbanized and relatively prosperous south and the much poorer rural north.

Nigeria is well aware of the importance of education in its development plans and has made recent policy statements stressing the important development function of schools in the rural areas. Nigeria has chosen to adopt an urban-based growth strategy, which essentially continues the colonial patterns of development, and since the early 1960s has been committed to a manpower planning approach to education supportive of this strategy. The stresses this has caused are all too apparent. There has been continual inflation, shortages of skilled tradesmen, engineers, managers and teachers (but a high rate of unemployment among school leavers), large-scale rural-urban migration and very little improvement in the agricultural sector.

Education is under the control of the central government but the states have a considerable responsibility and allocate about 30–40 per cent of their budgets to education. Nevertheless, Phillips (1975) gives the proportion of GNP spent on education to be not more than 3.2 per cent. The primary stage is seven years (6–12) but the proportion of children in this age group in school is almost certainly less than 34 per cent and 88 per cent of the population are recorded as illiterate.

Since independence it has been the aim of the Nigerian government to provide universal primary education (UPE) and immense efforts were made in the former Western and Eastern States to achieve this goal. Some writers regard their efforts as misguided, for so great a proportion of the states' revenue went on education that little was left for other forms of development, and, since the supply of schooled youngsters soon outstripped the capacity of the economy to absorb them, there was a severe unemployment problem. In the western area UPE has now been almost achieved, but in other areas the provision is still way below the hoped for level. Omojuwa (1977) reports that when the Primary Education Improvement Project (PEIP) started in the northern states with UNESCO and UNICEF aid in 1971, only 12 per cent of children were in school, only 39 per cent of the teachers had adequate qualifications and the majority of them lacked any post-primary education. Perhaps not surprisingly, teaching was judged to be poor and the materials inadequate. This project was apparently able to develop and improve the level of teaching in the schools that existed but it was clear to the author that only massive government funds could provide schooling for the majority of children in the northern states. The development of education in Nigeria is clearly linked to the preferred development strategy; in the prosperous (by African standards) industrial cities there is, virtually, universal primary education, and secondary provision for some 20 per cent of the children. But this development bypasses the rural north where only 10 per cent of the children are in primary school and only 1 per cent in secondary school. There is no real possibility of these imbalances being corrected. They can be understood as the results of a consciously pursued policy – and many observers are doubtful not only about the equity of such a policy, but of its effects on the long-term stability of Nigeria.

The discussion of rural-based minority cultures in chapter 6 concentrated on the position of the Welsh- and Gaelic-speaking peoples in Britain. Nigeria is a fairly representative example of the problems faced in this respect by LDCs. According to Aliyu (1977), there are about 200 mutually unintelligible languages in Nigeria; no one knows for certain since there are problems of definition involving the degree of intelligibility between dialects, but this can be taken as an approximate figure. The government decision in 1974 that all Nigerian children should be taught through their mother tongue in the initial stages and that one of the three major Nigerian languages, Ibo, Hausa or Oyo (Yoruba standard), should be introduced at a later primary stage in addition to English, is likely to make most educated

Nigerians trilingual and places considerable demand on teachers and pupils alike. In many areas where two languages are used in the community, most children grow up as bilinguals. A survey by Aliyu showed that 75 per cent of the children in his sample knew three languages (although not equally well), 12 per cent knew two languages and only 14 per cent were monoglots. The situation is, however, extremely variable. In areas where one of the three major African languages is used, English is learned as a second language. In certain other areas it has become traditionally accepted that minor language speakers will be taught through the medium of a major African language (Fulani speakers, for example, have long been taught through Hausa). Brann (1977) reports that in many areas a form of triglossa is normal: the mother tongue (or dialect of a major tongue) is used at home, a major Nigerian language is the medium of instruction in primary school and for internal business, and English is the medium for secondary and higher education and for national and international business. With the shortage of resources in Nigeria only limited attention can be given to the needs of minority linguistic groups, but some remarkably advanced projects have been carried out.

An account of the Isekiri project by Omamar (1977) is interesting in this context. After the new language policy in 1974 the University of Ibadan became involved with the development of Isekiri as a medium of education. The 1962 census enumerated some 100,000 Isekiri (although Otite (1975) gives the number as 530,000) in the Benin river and westernmost parts of the Niger delta regions. A language committee was formed with the task of collecting a vocabulary for a dictionary. Oral material, folk tales and so on, were collected for later transcription. At the same time work was initiated to produce a standard orthography. A set of initial primers was produced and a number of teachers attended a course where they learned to read and write Isekiri; these teachers then introduced the new primers to their schools. Competitions were held to encourage the submission of material in Isekiri for a collection of writing, and a monthly newsletter was published. Radio discussions, some in Isekiri, helped to popularize the scheme and inform local people of the developments. The project was run on a very small budget, the largest item being a special typewriter for Isekiri script. Omamar, commenting on the results, states that minority languages can only be the medium of instruction in schools if the language is first developed to meet the requirements of a teaching medium and that if the decision to introduce mother tongue instruction in the early primary stages is to be implemented, then these problems will have to be faced for a great number of minority languages in an effort which will call for appreciable funds.

Tanzania

Tanzania is the largest and most populous country in East Africa and has become one of the most closely observed countries on the continent. It is a poor country with few strategic reserves and there are no possibilities for rapid development. In 1974 income from two of its primary cash crops – cotton and sisal – was barely enough to pay for its oil imports. The mass of the population are near self-sufficient agriculturists producing only a small marketable surplus.

The earliest schools were established by German missionaries in the nineteenth century. The mission schools played an important part in the development of some of the remote areas and the provision of education in Tanzania, unlike most other African countries, is not greatly affected by the urban–rural distinction. The primary school cycle is seven years (7–13). Phillips (1975) gives the proportion of children in this age group at school as 34 per cent, but notes that this is likely to be an overestimate. More than 51 per cent of public expenditure goes on education, or about 4.5 per cent of GNP. The percentage of illiteracy is unknown but can safely be assumed to be high.

Education is more consciously linked to economic and social development in Tanzania than in many other states. The essential problem in Tanzanian development is to raise the living standards, and the marketable surplus, of the near self-sufficient farmers. Connell (1974) describes how after independence in 1961 the then Tanganyika adopted a World Bank plan to create large centralized villages of some 250 families, which would adopt the most modern farming methods based on mechanization and the high use of fertilizers. It was envisaged

131

that their prosperity would influence the surrounding neighbourhood to adopt similar methods. The plan failed. Over-capitalization created a crushing burden of debt, there were planning problems – inadequate water supplies and so on – and other difficuties, which led to a low level of morale amongst the villagers who quickly realized that these planned villages had reduced their standard of living. The failure of this policy had a profound effect on the future development of Tanzania. Nyerere (1967), in the Arusha declaration, laid the blame on a mistaken conception of modernization and proposed radical change:

> For the foreseeable future the vast majority of our people will continue to spend their lives in the rural areas and continue to work on the land. The land is the only basis for Tanzanian development; we have no other . . . . This means that we have to build up the countryside in such a way that our people have a better standard of living, while living together in terms of equality and fraternity. It also means that in the course of time, the advantages of town life in the way of services and personal pleasures and opportunities must become available to those who work in the rural sector as much as those in urban areas.

The change of direction in self-styled socialist Tanzania has been explicitly linked to the educational system which Nyerere regards as having had an essentially harmful effect on national development. He has criticized the educational system for being elitist and aiding the rise of a class structure, for divorcing people from the society to which they belonged, for denigrating, by its emphasis on book learning, traditional community knowledge and for being essentially parasitic on older and weaker persons whose work produces the wealth. He has stated that primary education could no longer be regarded in Tanzania as a preparatory stage for secondary education but must be sufficient as an education in itself. By the same token secondary education could not be regarded as a preparatory stage for university entrance but as leading to a life of service to the community. To this end the school curriculum must be thoroughly revised to reflect the needs of the rural economy and be integrated with the community. It is not enough for a school to possess a farm and a workshop, it must *be* a farm – a working community practising the principles of self-reliance and contributing to the development of the whole area. Phillips (1975) quotes Nyerere speaking at a UNESCO Conference in 1974:

> Parents, politicians, and workers, as well as educators, are suspicious of, or hostile to the educational innovations required. But the total result is that few of our schools are really an integral part of the village life, except in the sense that they occupy village children for so many hours a day.

Nyerere's criticisms of the educational system are brought out in Dubbledam's (1970) investigation of attitudes to education in Mwanza district on the southern shore of Lake Tanganyika. His survey showed that parents saw the school entirely as a means of access to urban employment, and were sceptical of the relevance of education to farm life. The higher grade teachers, in particular, placed farmers on the same level as carpenters and clerks, and far below professional occupations. These teachers identified with the life of the towns and not with the rural people among whom they lived. They saw their purpose as being to provide opportunities for personal advancement for their bright scholars and, even though there were very few secondary school places, regarded those who did not obtain a place as failures.

The policy of centralizing the villages and of improving the living standards and levels of production of the rural workers was not abandoned with the collapse of the World Bank scheme but was re-directed. The dependence on expensive outside capital was rejected in favour of a reliance on self-help community schemes which were intended to achieve essentially the same results. Economic self-reliance has proved difficult, but the aims of this policy have been achieved with 85 per cent of the population now living in 8,000 centralized villages. Although initially voluntary, 'villagification' was opposed by rich peasants and from 1973 onwards was completed by government direction. This enormous change in the structure of rural Tanzania (only 8 per cent of the population lived in villages in the early 1960s) has, as Raikes (1978) points out, important consequences for the extraction of peasant agricultural surplus by the urban

133

state class. Little is known about the fate of attempts to involve the schools in the development policy. Raikes' view is that practical education has proved to be no more than field drudgery, often used as a punishment, and has not affected the traditional function of the school, that is, to provide individual mobility for bright village boys. The indications are that the Tanzanian experiment, at least in respect of its educational aspirations, has failed, and if this is confirmed, it adds weight to those who have consistently argued that the school cannot be expected to alter society without changes in its political and social structure even more fundamental than those which have occurred in Tanzania.

Summary and conclusion

The problems of the developing world are immense. It is quite clear that countries without strategic resources cannot provide secondary education for more than a minority of their population and even universal primary education is probably beyond the reach of many countries. Moreover, it is realized that without continuing education for adults, and without newspapers and books – the infrastructure of literacy – many children will slip back into illiteracy. The central question is whether a country will develop a modern urbanized sector which holds its rural hinterland in a state of economic dependency (continues in fact the old colonial relationship) or whether it will attempt to build up the rural economy with the aim of equalizing living standards in all parts of the country. The part education has to play in that process will be determined by political and economic considerations which, fortunately or not, are only minimally the responsibility of educationists.

Regional and rural – problems for peripheries

It is a basic premise of this book that rural education cannot be adequately discussed with reference only to the obvious apparatus of the school system; its purposes can only be understood within the context of its relationship to the controlling institutions of the society in which it is situated. It has been consistently argued that for sociologists the relationship between rural and urban regions can be regarded as one characterized by dominance and power. This chapter examines the major sociological theories of rural and urban interdependence and their relevance to conditions of life in rural Britain.

Urban–rural interdependence

Buttell and Flinn (1977) have usefully reviewed three dominant theories of urban–rural interdependence: the Marxist, the Weberian and the Durkheimian. In what is still the most widely held view, which Buttell and Flinn argue convincingly is derived from Durkheimian functionalism, the backward periphery is gradually absorbed into the national system by the state apparatus of the dominant and superior culture of the urban centre, and, although its modernizing dynamic may be held up by the traditional values of unintegrated subcultures, its control of the central institutions eventually leads to the elimination of differences between urban and rural mentalities. Durkheim's concepts of mechanical and organic solidarity were mentioned briefly in chapter 1, and even a superficial knowledge of Durkheim's writings will reveal that Durkheim regarded the secular, urban-based nation state as the most progressive form of social organization. To him, organic solidarity was characteristic not of the village (where to our ears its use seems more appropriate), but the town. One might speculate on how close this is to normative practice in France. Of all European countries France is the most centre-dominated and the most uncompromising in its attitude toward the cultural aspirations of minority groups within its borders – the Bretons are the most obvious instance.

In contradistinction to this position modern Marxists (it is not the classical position and certainly not Marx's own) understand the urban–rural relationship as being based on the exploitation of the rural areas, typically, in creating a narrow specialized economy in the interests of metropolitan capital. The notion that urban life is progressive and rural life backward is rejected. Williams (1973), in a remarkable study informed by a broadly Marxist perspective, tells the long history of English rural society through an analysis of literary material.

Weberians (and Pahl might count as one) accept in general terms the effects on rural communities of urban dominance, but regard that dominance as being derived not only from economic power but from the possession of social power by urban-based elites who are able to gain and maintain control of the decisive institutions. This, of course, is Lipton's (1977) view, but it is not, as Buttell and Flinn argue, necessarily in opposition to the Marxist perspective, and elitist theories are increasingly regarded, by Wesolowski (1978) for example, as complementary to the neo-Marxist position.

This theoretical overview provides a necessary introduction to the discussion of uneven development which follows. Wales is a convenient case, statistics are readily available and its rural areas are doubly peripheral – peripheral to the Welsh urban industrial economy which in its turn is peripheral to the English urban industrial economy. It also happens that I have my home in the Welsh countryside and will be able to speak about something I know from personal experience. Pahl's (1966) observation, that the main issue for sociologists with an interest in the rural areas ought to be the relationship between the developed centre and the less developed periphery, has been taken up with some vigour by sociologists in Wales. To a considerable extent stimulated by Hechter (1975), who, as I mentioned briefly in chapter 8, sees Wales as an internal colony and places some importance on the ethnic division of labour, the discussion has become self-sustaining as it has drawn on the interest generated by the recent growth of political nationalism.

Rural Wales – a case study

All the indicators show that Wales is economically depressed by comparison with the rest of the United Kingdom and markedly so by comparison with the South East and Midlands regions. A few key indicators will illustrate the extent of this depression. The Welsh per capita GNP was £1,104 in 1974, that is 83.9 per cent of the UK average and the lowest regional figure, excepting the even more depressed Northern Ireland, and can be compared with 116.6 per cent in the South East region. During the decade 1965–75 male employment declined by 13 per cent, compared with an average UK decline of 9 per cent, while female employment (thought to reflect the tendency for women to seek part-time work in an attempt to maintain the level of family income) rose by 19 per cent, compared with a UK average of 12 per cent. Unemployment in 1976 was 6.9 per cent, or 1.3 times the national average. Average male earning were 97 per cent of the UK average and the female earnings 98.5 per cent.

Wales has, from the earliest times, been dependent upon its powerful neighbour. In the Middle Ages cattle and wool were produced for the English market but the surplus value from this trade was invested elsewhere, notably in the fine houses of the merchants in Shrewsbury and London. Later industrial

137

development concentrated on the primary and extractive sector – coal, slate, water – and where other industries were established, for example, tin plate – 90 per cent of which was manufactured in and around Llanelli – the product was typically finished elsewhere. Most of the profits of these industries went outside Wales, and no self-supporting industrial base was created around them. A classic instance occurred in North Wales where local capital developed the slate quarries (and reduced a class of smallholders and tenant farmers to wage labourers), but the great fortunes generated from this industry were not reinvested, but lost in conspicuous consumption.

The over-specialization of the Welsh economy emphasized its vulnerability in the period 1921–39 when nearly half-a-million people, half of them aged between fifteen and twenty-nine, left Wales leaving a depopulated countryside, a moribund economy and heavy long-term unemployment in the industrialized areas. The second war, which brought the strategic re-siting of some manufacturing industry to South Wales, seems to have been the economic salvation of Wales. Unemployment in the great slump of the 1930s was nowhere higher than in Wales. In 1929, 19.3 per cent of registered workers were unemployed, the figures rose to 36.5 per cent in 1932 and declined slowly to 25.9 per cent in 1938. By 1949 it was at only 4 per cent and stayed below that until 1967, since when the figures have tended to rise. This is an unquestioned improvement but it needs to be supplemented by other figures. Industrial productivity grew more rapidly in Wales in the post-war period than in Britain as a whole, as a major structural change occurred in the Welsh industrial base. Its dependence on extractive industry disappeared; the number of workers employed in mining and quarrying fell from 290,000 in 1931 to 52,000 in 1970, while during the same period the number in manufacturing rose from 117,000 to 254,000. These figures for Wales as a whole are more illustrative of the industrial than the rural sector of the economy, but even in rural Radnorshire the number of persons engaged in manufacturing rose from 10 per cent in 1961, to 22 per cent in 1971; although this did little, of course, to absorb the loss from employment in agriculture which, in that county, fell from 40 per cent to 28 per cent in the same decade. These changes were coupled with a decline in agricultural employment and a rise in professional and scientific services. It might be worth noting in passing that Khleif's hypothesis about the rise of a Welsh professional class is thus not unsupported by the evidence. During the post-war period the long depopulation of Wales went into reverse – from a loss of 49,000 in 1951–61, down to a mere 4,000 in 1961–7 and during the period of 1971–3 an actual rise of 17,000.

A closer analysis shows that in the two decades 1951–61 and 1961–71, 44 per cent of Welsh rural parishes lost population continuously and in 6.8 per cent earlier growth was reversed in the later decade, implying a population loss in 50.8 per cent of Welsh rural parishes during 1961–71. At the same time, 25.5 per cent gained population throughout these decades, and as many as 23.7 per cent reversed earlier depopulation in the latter decade. These changes can be seen to be influenced by urban development and are a result of either local industrial development or housing development related to more distant industry; in brief, the remoter areas have continued to decline – many of them more sharply.

The most intense problems have been experienced by mid-Wales. This large area, about half the size of Wales, has 10 per cent of the population, a population which has declined from 215,492 in 1911, to 174,089 in 1971. The low density of population, the decline of marginal agriculture, the low levels of income, the dispersal of families and community frustration at loss of services (buses, shops, small tradesmen, etc.) has been a concern to the authorities in the post-war period. A Welsh Office Report (1964) describes the effects of this process:

> The results of this denudation has been to leave a residue, a high proportion of whom, particularly amongst the small owner-occupier farms, can be regarded as marginal . . . in the sense that they would meet further economic adversity by reducing yet lower their standard of living. Thus one of the main consequences of outward migration has been to produce this hard core of the farming community, lacking in financial resources and supported by a minority of secondary population and isolated miscellaneous groups, many of whom suffer from the same deficiencies.

The social results of this depopulation and underdevelopment have been sharply felt in Gwynedd. The third smallest county in terms of population, its long history of out-migration has left a deficit in the 15–44 age group, and a surplus in the 60–65 plus age group which is exaggerated by the in-migration of economically inactive persons in this group. The rise in the number of part-time women workers has led to their being unavailable for extended family roles and has led to increased demand on social services. It is estimated that Gwynedd will need to double its case-carrying social work staff and home help service in order to cope with the new problems created by these structural conditions.

The results of this process are brought forcibly to the attention of politicians and administrators by people suffering them, and solutions are generally sought from two areas of professional expertise: economic development and town and country planning.

Regionalism

Regional policies have been motivated by the need to correct regional imbalance for several reasons. Gilg (1976) lists six: unequal standards of living produce political (and nationalist) dissension and are unacceptable in terms of the accepted socio-political rhetoric; agricultural employment cannot support communities of an economic size, implying a need for alternative employment; there is a need to utilize reserves of labour which if brought into production could aid economic prosperity; the exodus of people to urban areas creates congestion and puts strain on existing services; the social capital in rural areas is expensive to replace once lost; and, finally, most people don't want to leave and it is unacceptable to allow economic forces to make them.

Conventional development theory is based on the notion that centres of production will create not only immediate employment in manufacturing industry but will have a multiplier effect as wages are spent to create further local employment in services. This 'trickle down' is an important factor in stimulating further growth. Its assumptions have been criticized by some orthodox economists, notably Myrdal (1957) who argues that once regional differences have been created they are likely to become increasingly wide, as well-established areas generate new ideas and capital, creating self-sustained internal development, and thus inevitably weakening other areas by the emigration of the most enterprising labour. But regional policy is firmly established in Britain, and has long been the cornerstone of government policy in relation to the less developed regions. An official view is given in an OECD Report (1976) which briefly relates the reasons for regional differences in Britain to the historical development of British industry and gives a detailed account of the development of regional policy from its beginning in 1934 to mid-1973, when all Wales, Scotland, Northern Ireland and most of Northern England had development area status of one kind or another, and were in receipt of nearly £400 million in grants. In all, about 1.3 million jobs in the 'old' sector of the economy have been lost in these areas since 1945 and about 30 per cent of these have been replaced with jobs in other industries.

A major impact of regional policy has been made through the new towns. Since 1946 some 800,000 people have been resettled in new towns. One of the most interesting, in the context of the discussion about mid-Wales, is the development of Newtown. The Council for Wales was instrumental in gaining development status for seven towns in mid-Wales and this policy has had some effect in that six of the seven towns have grown, though at the expense of the outlying parishes which have declined by 2.5 per cent during the decade ending 1971. However, the greatest effort has gone into the development of Newtown. Newtown was the second largest town in the mid-Wales area, the nearest to the Midlands, with better lines of communication than the others and it already had some manufacturing industry. The Newtown Development Corporation was established in 1968 with the plan of attracting manufacturing industry and doubling the size of the town to 11–13,000 within a decade. The efforts of the Development Corporation have been successful in that industry has been attracted (though not in the dynamic sectors of the economy) and there has been no difficulty in attracting workers to live in a small town. About 40 per

141

cent of the new inhabitants are from Wales while half of the remainder are from the Midlands. There is not a significantly high number of returners and the majority of in-migrants settle down to stay. There are some dissatisfactions at the lack of overtime and restricted job opportunities (particularly for their children), but Morgan (1977) found that 80 per cent of the sample of Newtown migrants he interviewed were satisfied with their move – although less than half thought they had improved their standard of living. Although the Newtown Development Corporation has been successful in its immediate aims it is open to question whether the strategic objectives have been achieved; unemployment is higher in mid-Wales now than ten years ago and income levels are still below those in the rest of the UK. Nor is it obvious that the multiplier effect has made an appreciable difference to the position of mid-Wales. Some regard this as due to the inherent contradictions of the development strategy, others regard it as being due to undercapitalized or insufficiently rapid growth.

There are obvious contradictions in the theory of regional development. Even by the government's own admission its policy has been responsible for no more than a 30 per cent replacement of the loss of jobs in the declining sectors. Morgan (1978) argues, that since the essential role of the state at the macro-economic level is to stimulate production and profit – 'growth' – it is not in competition with capital and, consequently, in no position to interfere in a more than marginal sense with the tendency of capital to move into the most buoyant sectors of the economy and the most active regions. Conventional regional theory is clearly under stress. More than half the country now has development or special development status but the problems remain and, indeed, worsen. Fortunately, governments in a democratic state have pressures other than those of capital to which they must respond – in this case unemployment – which do to some extent allow it to act as a countervailing power against economic imperatives. The crises in the Western economies is such, however, that the search for manufacturing jobs becomes increasingly difficult. Additionally, there is the permanent problem of technological unemployment which has reduced manufacturing jobs in the UK from 8.4 million to 7.7

million between 1966 and 1974, and the process is gaining momentum. The competition for capital is thus becoming more intense and increasingly crippling conditions have to be met. One in six manufacturing jobs in Wales are in foreign-owned firms who have been attracted to Wales by tax inducements, high depreciation allowances and relative freedom from wage control. The profits from these enterprises are, of course, transferred abroad and are thus not available for reinvestment in Wales except on similar terms. This makes their products increasingly competitive with British-based firms and, as a policy, is obviously two-edged. Moreover, foreign-owned 'branch' establishments are highly capital intensive thus requiring relatively little labour and are vulnerable to closure in times of severe recession. In the view of many observers, for example Fletcher (1978), the present situation also offers good pickings for fly-by-night operators who can make more from government grants than from legitimate trading profits.

Morgan sees the problem of uneven development as merely a geographical restatement of class relationships. Capitalism in this view is characterized by uneven development at all levels. Some economic sectors grow at the expense of others, some classes grow in wealth and power at the expense of others, some regions develop at the expense of others and, finally, some countries develop at the expense of others. Uneven development is thus seen as an inevitable consequence of capitalist economic forces and only marginally open to correction by government intervention. Morgan writes: 'Uneven spatial development is the reflection in geographic space of the uneven movements of capital through those sectors which yield above or average rates of profit . . .' Low levels of profit and production have led to a preoccupation with the international condition of capitalism and also to a concern with the problem in specific regions which are seen as problem areas. Morgan argues the need to relate these together and to investigate the mechanisms which generate uneven development.

Town and country planning

All the indications are that the answer to rural depopulation, certainly in the remote areas, is not to be sought through increasingly hard to attract capital investment in manufacturing. The town and country planning perspective on rural problems is not so much on the question of economic development but on the re-shaping and redistribution of settlement patterns. The early concerns of town and country planning were with the preservation of the green belt as a *cordon sanitaire* around the growing towns and cities of the early twentieth century in the attempt to prevent ribbon development and uncontrolled urban sprawl. Town and country planning received its post-war impetus with the Agriculture Act 1947, the Town and Country Planning Act 1947 and the National Parks and Access to the Countryside Act 1949. City growth has gone through several stages. During the 1890s and onwards the movement of the railway network brought the suburbanization of Middlesex and the greater parts of Surrey, Hertfordshire and Essex. The private car from the 1920s onwards, and rapidly in the 1950s, made further outward movement possible and saw the suburbanization of villages within twenty to thirty miles of large cities. The network of motorways has produced its own version of ribbon development as villages and small towns fifty or more miles from a metropolitan area become accessible. This movement has brought great changes to the countryside.

A study of Norfolk villages reported by Green (1971), found that 30 per cent of the people had lived there for less than five years, the proportion of adults born in the village was rarely more than 40 per cent and an average of half the working population travelled out of the village to work each day. The Hampshire County Council Survey (1966) revealed the same pattern. To the surprise of the planners, the villages had the same proportion of people born there, 19 per cent, as in the town, 21 per cent. And village people travelled more-or-less the same distance to work as did those in town. The only observable difference was in the proportion of cars which proved to be higher in the rural areas. Most of those who had moved into the countryside did so for reasons of greater peace and quiet and a more natural setting in which to live; the movement from town to country is almost always in search of better or cheaper housing and to escape the noise and other problems associated with

144

urban life. The new suburbs and the expanded villages have much in common. Inhabitants expect to find shops, schools, recreation facilities and adequate transport. There is, in addition, the substantial movement of retired persons into the countryside, although not necessarily to the same villages as commuters.

Modern country planning is based on central place theory. Originally developed by Christaller (1966) this has been the cornerstone of town and country planning for many years – put simply it means that planners recognize the need to take into account the various levels of services located in towns of different sizes and to ensure that all settlements are within range of one or more central places where such services can be obtained. In practice it has become identified with the 'key' village system. A Cambridgeshire survey showed that villages of the following sizes could expect to have these levels of services:

170 – 600:	shop, post office, public house
600 – 1,100:	the above and a primary school, playing field and a garage
1,100 – 1,800:	the above and a police house, doctor, butcher and ladies hairdresser
1,800 – 3,000:	the above and an electrical shop, hardware store, licenced club and gents hairdresser
3,000 plus:	the above plus a secondary school and a chemist

A similar study in Norfolk of village facilities suggested that the appropriate level would be one district nurse or health visitor for every four to five villages, a group surgery for every six to seven villages, a junior school for every six to ten villages, and a range of shopping facilities in only ten villages. The population regarded as necessary to support a viable rural community is around 2,000-5,000. This immediately causes conflict for the overwhelming evidence is that people prefer communities of between 700 to 1,000, with 1,500 as an upper limit. Green (1971), who reports several similar studies, writes with chilling observance of the planners' main point of reference: 'There are too many villages which by any measure of cost against benefit, are too small . . .' The solution in planning terms is the 'key'

145

village. Certain villages chosen for their central location and possession of a reasonably good infrastructure – sewerage, water, electricity, school, bus service, etc. – will be allowed to develop and the rest will not. In this way people will be forced to live in centralized villages and not elsewhere.

Planners are aware that the general level of population in the countryside is declining. The decrease in agricultural workers is about 4 per cent a year and in the view of agricultural economists is not finished yet. The farming industry and ancillary trades are likely to provide employment for no more than twenty-five persons per square mile and, with a threshold population of 2,000 as the minimum viable village in planning terms, that implies a countryside deserted but for isolated farmhouses and a few very large 'key' villages on the main roads. The arithmetic implies a tract of countryside fifteen miles square (that is 225 square miles) with just one village of about 2,500 people, assuming that about half the population will be living on outlying farms. Even if we include a substantial percentage of non-farming population the picture is not greatly improved. Not surprisingly, this is a horrific vision to anyone outside a planning department. The Director of the Council for the Protection of Rural England has no doubts about the dangers of the 'key' village policy: 'The effect of this "key" village policy is to create a spiral of decline in the villages not selected for growth.' It is a policy which clearly implies the decline of some villages and the disfigurement of others by suburbanization. Planners are a particularly embattled group and are regarded with open suspicion by many country people who have not been impressed by what they take to be the results of urban planning in the cities and are apprehensive of the attentions of planners being turned to their areas. The unconcealed cost-consciousness of planners is, in fact, all too likely to lead to a repetition of the sorts of mistakes that were made in the cities and is particularly disturbing. The Devonshire County Council Development Plan Survey quoted by Woodruffe (1976) for example, states that its policy is: 'to secure the most economic distribution of public utilities including gas, water, electricity, sewerage, telephone, postal services and social services such as schools.' The inclusion of schools in this list confirms the suspicions of many observers that it is the economic viability of the small school, rather than its educational viability, that is the real reason for school amalgamation policies. It may be no accident that two counties noted for their high number of school closures – Devon and Cambridgeshire – are authorities which have particularly active and influential planning departments.

The criticism of conventional planning solutions have led to an awareness on the part of some villagers to develop their own solutions. This has led to several interesting developments. In the field of transport new alternatives to uneconomic stage-carriage services are being experimented with. The Scottish post-bus service, probably the most successful of these, carries thousands of passengers a year. Clwyd are especially active in supporting alternative transport schemes. In Gwynedd the villagers of Llanelhearn have formed a co-operative which has attracted a small factory to the village and has also produced and marketed knitwear and pottery for the tourist trade. Village organizations such as the Women's Institute are being encouraged by the Council for the Protection of Rural England to make their own planning surveys, not necessarily in opposition to the county planners, but certainly to supplement their perspective and to ensure that local opinion is understood.

The future of rural life is at a particularly critical stage for it is not at all certain which way the future lies. The countryside could depopulate outside the commuting radius of large cities and become the desert orthodox planning threatens to create and as Dunn (1976) fears:

> The forecast . . . is one of continuing polarization in population change in the rural areas of Britain, with further losses and resultant cuts in services, withdrawal of support, and so on, from the remoter areas, and the further suburbanization of the accessible countryside, with the spread of urban decentralization held in check only by unsatisfactory controls in green belts and landscape protection and by the imperfect process of development control . . . The wave of structure planning currently breaking over rural Britain has shown little sign of innovatory approaches to persistent problems. Faith is still placed in key villages to shore up stagnant and declining areas, despite the effect upon the remaining major-

ity of settlements, and despite evidence that settlement reorganization is of strictly limited value in population retention.

Or it could become revitalized by increasing in-migration. There are signs of a movement into the countryside by that section of the middle class which for the last forty years has been content with a suburban life, and though oil shortages are eventually bound to affect long-distance commuting by car, there could still be time for a marked growth in this trend. Technological changes may become important and the development of communications has meant that an increasing number of people are able to sever the geographical connection between their place of work and their place of residence. Many self-employed and other employed people find they can do the greater part of their work at or from home. They include accountants, writers, draughtsmen, commercial artists, craftsmen, travellers of all kinds, including representatives and service engineers, and so on. In addition, there are an increasing number of highly paid professional workers, lecturers, surgeons, and self-employed businessmen of all kinds, who find it unnecessary to work – at least in a central place – for more than two or three days a week. So people who might once have driven out to a weekend cottage now find they can live in the cottage and drive out to work for a few days mid-week. The tape cassette, the dictaphone, the telex, all help to make this possible. Further developments in telecommunications will increase the viability of this way of life and could significantly alter the structure of all but the remotest areas.

Summary and conclusion

The rural–urban distinction is clearly more than a descriptive label for land with houses and land without houses. The relationships between centre and periphery, and town and country are shown to be in a continual state of tension. Recent writers, Williams (1973) and Lipton (1977), have shown that this relationship has always been an unequal one in which the resources of the countryside and the regions have been exploited for the benefit of the urban population. The position of Wales in Britain enables us to examine both the effects of economic dependency at a national level and the internal effects of industrial development on declining rural areas. Neither conventional economic planning nor conventional town and country planning are likely to substantially moderate the effects of the market forces which continue to depopulate the remote rural areas.

Sociological theories of urban–rural interdependence have not been articulated with concepts of regional or countryside planning but it does appear that both may be shifting from what was described as the Durkheimian view, that rural areas are naturally undynamic, to the Weberian view, that they are exposed to exploitation by powerful urban forces. Dunn's comments quoted above are an example of the changing mood.

The implications for education are not easy to determine. But, in the first place, if the remote areas continue to decline then the attitude of planners, that schools shall be considered only in terms of their economic viability as public utilities, must be challenged if our aim is to support and encourage living communities. Second, more attention may need to be given to the structure of courses in the secondary school; it might be possible for schools to have a more positive involvement – as the best village colleges do – in the life of their area. One of the reasons for the success of the bilingual schools in Wales is almost certainly due to their deep involvement with the culture of the community. And, if young adults gained an understanding of the social forces structuring their lives through their participation in the community, we might see the start of more thorough-going changes in social attitudes towards rural life.

References and
name index

The numbers in italics after each entry refer to page numbers within this book.

Adams, D. (1977) Development education. *Comparative Education Review 21*, 2, 3: 296–310. *121*

Aliyu, J.S. (1977) The problems of multi-lingualism in Nigerian primary and post-primary schools. Kaduna Language Symposium, Nigeria (mimeo). *129*

Anderson, C.A. and Bowman, M.J. (eds) (1965) *Education and Economic Development*. Chicago: Aldine. *121*

Barker, R. and Gump, P.V. (1964) *Big School, Small School*. Berkeley: University of California Press. *72*

Barr, F. (1959) Urban and rural differences in ability and attainment. *Educational Research 1*, 2: 49–50. *36*

Barth, F. (ed.) (1959) *Ethnic Groups and Boundaries*. Boston: Little, Brown. *85*

Bauer, P.T. (1976) *Dissent on Development*. London: Weidenfeld & Nicolson. *117*

Bauser, J. (1978) A better way to teach and learn. *ILEA Contact 1*: 18–20. *74*

Bell, W. (1974) Comparative research on ethnicity: a conference report. *SSRC Council Items 28. 85*

Bell, C. and Newby, H. (eds) (1974) *The Sociology of Community: A Selection of Readings*. London: Frank Cass. *13*

Benford, M. (1978) Village school priorities. *Where 136*: 78–80. *66*

Benn, C. and Simon, B. (1970) *Half-way There*. New York: McGraw-Hill. *71*

Bessant, B. (1978) Rural schooling and the rural myth in Australia.

Comparative Education 14, 2: 121–8. *51*

Boal, F.W. (1974) Territoriality in Belfast. In C. Bell and H. Newby (eds) *The Sociology of Community: A Selection of Readings*. London: Frank Cass. *41*

Board of Education (1934) *Education and the Countryside*. London: HMSO. *29*

Board of Education (Welsh Department) (1947) *Education in Rural Wales*. Cardiff: HMSO. *31*

Bourdieu, P. and Passeron, J.C. (1977) *Reproduction in Education, Society and Culture*. London: Sage Publications. *50, 125*

Bourhis, R.Y., Giles, H. and Tajfel, H. (1973) Language as a determinant of Welsh identity. *European Journal of Social Psychology 3*: 447–60. *84*

Brann, C.M.B. (1977) Triglossia in Nigerian education. Kaduna Language Symposium, Nigeria (mimeo). *130*

Brimer, M.A. and Pauli, L. (1971) *Wastage in Education, a World Problem*. New York: UNESCO. *123*

Butler, K. and Morgan, C. (1966) Village colleges re-examined. *Adult Education 17*: 15–20. *24*

Buttell, F.H. and Flinn, W.C. (1977) The interdependence of rural and urban environmental problems in advanced capitalist societies: models of linkage. *Sociologia Ruralis 17*, 4: 255–81. *135*

Byrne, D., Williamson, B. and Fletcher, B. (1975) *The Poverty of Education*. London: Martin Robertson. *28*

Cadbury, P.S. (1974) *The Chapmans Hill School Farm Experiment*. London: Association of Agriculture. *33*

Campbell, W.J. (ed.) (1970) *Scholars in Context*. Chichester: John Wiley. *72*

Central Advisory Council for Education (Wales) (1960) *Education in Rural Wales*. Cardiff: HMSO. *31*

Centre for Information on Language Teaching and Research (1976) *Bilingualism and British Education: The Dimensions of Diversity*. London: CILT Reports and Papers 14. *87*

Christaller, W.C. (1966) *Central Places in Southern Germany*. Englewood Cliffs, NJ: Prentice-Hall. *145*

Cogan, M. and van der Eyken, W. *et al*. (1973) *County Hall: The Role of the Chief Education Officer*. Harmondsworth: Penguin. *55*

Connell, J. (1974) *The Evolution of Tanzanian Rural Development*. Brighton: Institute of Development Studies, University of Sussex. *131*

David, M. (1976) Size and education. Bristol: Department of Social

Administration, University of Bristol (mimeo). *74*

Davies, W. (1962) Challenge of the small rural school. *The Teacher in Wales* Aug./Sept.: 15–17; Oct.: 9–11. *54*

Day, G. (1977) Key issues in the sociology of Wales. Aberystwyth: Department of Sociology and Social Anthropology, University College of Wales, Aberystwyth (mimeo). *17*

Department of Education and Science (1961, 1976) *Statistics of Education*. London: HMSO. *55*

Douglas, J.W.B. *et al.* (1968) *All Our Future*. London: Peter Davies. *38*

Dubbledam, L.F.B. (1970) *The Primary School and the Community in Mwanze District Tanzania*. Groningen: Wolters Noordhoff. *133*

Dumont, R. (1963) *False Start in Africa*. London: André Deutsch. *119*

Dumont, R. and Wax, M. (1976) Cherokee school society and the intercultural classroom. In J. Beck, C. Jenks, N. Keddie and M.F.D. Young (eds) *Worlds Apart: Readings for a Sociology of Education*. London: Collier Macmillan. *39*

Dunn, M.C. (1976) Population change and settlement pattern. In G. Cherry (ed.) *Rural Planning Problems*. London: Leonard Hill. *147*

Durkacz, V. (1977) Gaelic education in the nineteenth century. *Scottish Educational Review* 9, 1: 18–28. *96*

Durkheim, E. (1972) *Selected Writings*. Translated and edited by A. Giddens. Cambridge: Cambridge University Press. *14*

Emmett, I. (1964) *A North Wales Village: A Social Anthropological Study*. London: Routledge & Kegan Paul. *13*

Evans, L.W. (1974) *Studies in Welsh Education*. Cardiff: University of Wales Press. *91*

Fishman, J.A. (1976) *Bilingual Education*. Rowley, Mass: Newbury House. *86*

Fletcher, C. (1978) Regional community and the era of regional aid. In G. Williams (ed.) *Social and Cultural Change in Contemporary Wales*. London: Routledge & Kegan Paul. *143*

Foster, P. (1965) The vocational school fallacy in development planning. In C.A. Anderson and M.J. Bowman (eds) *Education and Economic Development*. Chicago: Aldine. *125*

Foster, P. (1975) Dilemmas of educational development: What we might learn from the past. *Comparative Education Review 19*, 2, 3: 375–92. *124*

Foster, P. (1977) Education and social differentiation in less developed countries. *Comparative Education Review 21*, 2, 3: 211–29. *121*

Frank, A.G. (1971) The sociology of development and the underdevelopment of sociology. In J.D. Cockcroft *et al.* (eds) *Dependence and Underdevelopment*. New York: Anchor Books. *117*

Frankenberg, R. (1966) *Communities in Britain: Social Life in Town and Country*. Harmondsworth: Penguin. *13*

Garvey, A. (1976) Closing down the village schools. *Where 119*: 204–7. *16, 59*

Giles, H. (ed.) (1977) *Language, Ethnicity and Intergroup Relations*. London: Academic Press. *84, 87*

Gilg, A. (1976) Rural employment. In G. Cherry (ed.) *Rural Planning Problems*. London: Leonard Hill. *140*

Gittins Report (1968) *Primary Education in Wales*. Cardiff: HMSO. *53, 67, 93*

Goldthorpe, J.E. (1975) *The Sociology of the Third World, Disparity and Involvement*. Cambridge: Cambridge University Press. *118, 122*

Grant, N. (1977) Educational policy and cultural pluralism: a task for comparative education. *Comparative Education 13*, 2: 139–50. *87*

Green, R.J. (1971) *Country Planning: the Future of the Rural Regions*. Manchester: Manchester University Press. *144, 145*

Halsall, E. (1973) *The Comprehensive School: Guidelines to the Reorganisation of Secondary Education*. Oxford: Pergamon. *72, 74, 76*

Hamilton, D.(1973) Big science, small school. Paper presented to a symposium of the 34th Annual Meeting of the Society for Applied Anthropology, Royal Tropical Institute, Amsterdam (mimeo). *82*

Hampshire County Council (1966) *Village Life in Hampshire*. Winchester. *144*

Harbison, F.H. (1973) *Human Resources as the Wealth of Nations*. London: Oxford University Press. *121*

Hechter, M. (1975) *Internal Colonialism: The Case of Wales*. Berkeley: University of California Press. *86, 137*

Hilton, A.C. and Audric, J.E. (1946) *The School Farm*. London: Harrap. *30*

Hirschman, A. (1958) *The Strategy of Economic Development*. New Haven, Conn.: Yale University Press. *119*

Høgms, A. and Solstad, K.J. (1977) The Lofoten Project: towards a relevant education. Interskola Report. Norwich: Keswick Hall College of Education. *109*

Hoogvelt, A.M.M. (1976) *The Sociology of Developing Societies*. London: Macmillan. *117*

House of Commons (1847) Report of the Commissioners of Enquiry into the State of Education in Wales. *89*

Illich, I. (1972) *Deschooling Society*. Harmondsworth: Penguin. *122*

Inkeles, A. and Smith, D.H. (1974) *Becoming Modern*. Cambridge, Mass: Harvard University Press. *122*

James Report (1972) *Teacher Education and Training*. London: HMSO. *103*

Jolly, R. (1971) Contrast in Cuban and African educational stategies. In J. Lowe, N. Grant and T.D. Williams (eds) *Education and Nation Building in the Third World*. Edinburgh: Scottish Academic Press. *123*

Jones, J.H. (1961) Can the village school survive? *The Teacher in Wales* Feb.: 7–9. *55*

Keddie, N. (ed.) (1973) *Tinker, Tailor . . . the Myth of Cultural Deprivation*. Harmondsworth: Penguin. *122*

Khleif, B.B. (1975) Cultural regeneration and the schools: an anthropological study of Welsh-medium schools in Wales. Durham, New Hampshire: Department of Sociology and Anthropology, University of New Hampshire (mimeo). *92*

Khleif, B.B. (1978) Ethnic awakening in the First World: the case of Wales. In G. Williams (ed.) *Social and Cultural Change in Contemporary Wales*. London: Routledge & Kegan Paul. *92*

Knox, P.L. (1975) *Social Well-Being: A Spatial Perspective*. Oxford: Oxford University Press. *43*

Lerew, V. (1976) Wigton Teachers' Centre. Cumbria LEA (mimeo). *104–5*

Lewes, E.G. (1977) Modernisation and language maintenance. Paper presented to the Gregynog Conference on Social and Cultural Change in Contemporary Wales (mimeo). *94*

Lindbekk, T. (1969) Ecological factors and educational performance. In M.A. Matthijssen and C.E. Vervoort (eds) *Education in Europe: Sociological Research*. The Hague: Mouton. *107*

Lipton, M. (1977) *Why Poor People Stay Poor*. London: Maurice Temple Smith. *117, 124, 125, 136, 148*

Littlejohn, J. (1963) *Westrigg: The Sociology of a Cheviot Parish*. London: Routledge & Kegan Paul. *13*

Lloyd, G. (1978) *Deprivation and the Bilingual Child*. Schools Council Research Studies. Oxford: Blackwell and Department of Education, Swansea. *46*

Lynd, R.S. and Lynd, H.M. (1929) *Middletown: A Study in Contemporary American Culture*. New York: Harcourt Brace. *13*

Lynd, R.S. and Lynd, H.M. (1937) *Middletown in Transition*. New York: Harcourt Brace. *13*

McDonald, B. and Walker, R. (1976) *Changing the Curriculum*. London: Open Books. *127*

MacKinnon, K. (1977) *Language, Education and Social Processes in a Gaelic Community*. London: Routledge & Kegan Paul. *96*

MacLeod, F. (1977) The Western Islands community education project. Interskola Report. Norwich: Keswick Hall College of Education. *105*

MacNamara, J.T. (1966) *Bilingualism and Primary Education*. Edinburgh: Scottish University Press. *88*

McVeagh, H. (1977) *Schoolroom in the Home*. Wellington: Department of Education. *113*

Malassis, L. (1976) *The Rural World*. London: Croom Helm. *124*

Mason, J. (1936) *A History of Scottish Experiments in Rural Education*. London: University Press. *21*

Ministry of Education (1958) *Schools and the Countryside*. London: HMSO. *29*

Ministry of Overseas Development (1970) *Education in Developing Countries*. London: HMSO. *124*

Monks, T.G. (1968) *Comprehensive Education in England and Wales*. Slough: National Foundation for Educational Research. *73, 94*

Morgan, K. (1978) Capital, the state and regional planning: a framework for analysis. Paper presented to the Gregynog Conference on Social and Cultural Change in Contemporary Wales (mimeo). *142*

Morgan, R.H. (1977) Population trends in Mid-Wales: some policy implications. Paper presented to the Gregynog Conference on Social and Cultural Change in Contemporary Wales (mimeo). *142*

Myrdal, G. (1957) *Economic Theory and Underdeveloped Regions*. London: Duckworth. *141*

Myrdal, G. (1968) *Asian Drama: An Inquiry into the Poverty of Nations*. New York: Pantheon. *122*

Nash, R., Williams, H. Ll. and Evans, M. (1976) The one-teacher school. *British Journal of Educational Studies 24*, 1: 12–32. *67*

Nash, R. (1977) Village schools in North Wales: their educational, social and economic viability. A Report to the Social Science Research Council and the Welsh Education Office. *60*

National Foundation for Educational Research (1961) *National Survey of Attainments*. Slough: NFER. *37*

Newby, H. (1977) *The Deferential Worker: A Study of Farm Workers in East Anglia*. London: Allen Lane. *52*

Nurske, R. (1970) The conflict between 'balanced growth' and international specialisation. In G.M. Meier (ed.) *Leading Issues in Eco-*

nomic Development. London and New York: Oxford University Press. *119*

Nyerere, J. (1967) *Socialism and Rural Development.* Dar es Salaam: Government Printer. *132*

Ogionwo, W. (1969) The adoption of technological innovation in Nigeria: a study of factors associated with the adoption of farm practices. Ph.D. thesis, University of Leeds. *122*

Omamar, A.P. (1977) Towards mother tongue education: a case study of the Isekiri language project. Kaduna Language Symposium, Nigeria (mimeo). *130*

Omojuwa, R.A. (1977) Problems in language planning for bilingual education at the primary education level with particular reference to Nigeria's Northern States' situation. Kaduna Language Symposium, Nigeria (mimeo). *129*

Organization for Economic Co-operation and Development (1976) *Regional Problems and Policies in OECD Countries.* Vol. 2. Paris. *107, 141*

Otite, O. (1975) Resource competition and inter-ethnic relations in Nigeria. In L.A. Despres (ed.) *Ethnicity and Resource Competition in Plural Societies.* The Hague: Mouton. *130*

Owen, J.G. (1977) *The Planning of Alternative Pre-School Arrangements in an Area Where Few Pre-School Establishments Exist: Devon in the United Kingdom.* Paris: Council for Cultural Co-operation, OECD. *44*

Pahl, R.E. (1964) Urbs in rure: the metropolitan fringe in Hertfordshire. London: London School of Economics and Political Science, Geographical Papers No. 2. *14*

Pahl, R.E. (1966) The rural urban continuum. *Sociologia Ruralis 6:* 299–329. *15, 17, 38, 137*

Paulston, R.G. (1974) *Folk High Schools in Social Change: A Partisan Guide to the International Literature.* Pittsburgh: University of Pittsburgh Press. *110*

Phillips, H.M. (1975) *Basic Education- a World Challenge.* London: John Wiley. *122, 128, 131, 133*

Plowden Report (1967) *Children and their Primary Schools.* London: HMSO. *39, 40, 53, 54*

Raikes, P. (1978) Rural differentiation and class formation in Tanzania. *Journal of Peasant Societies 5,* 3: 285–325. *133*

Redfield, R. (1968) *The Primitive World and its Transformations.* Harmondsworth: Penguin. *14*

Ree, H. (1973) *Educator Extraordinary: The Life and Achievements of Henry Morris 1889–1961*. London: Longman. *22*

Robbins Report (1963) *Higher Education*. London: HMSO. *28*

Robinson, P. (1976) *Education and Poverty*. London: Methuen. *39*

Roebuck, M., Bloomer, J. and Hamilton, D. (1974) Independent learning materials and science teaching in small schools in the Highlands and Islands of Scotland. Glasgow: Department of Education, University of Glasgow (mimeo). *79*

Rogers, R. (1977) Closing the village schools: what the LEAs are up to. *Where 133*: 276–80. *77*

Rolls, M.J. (1965) Some aspects of rural education in England and Wales. *Comparative Education Review 9*: 177–85. *29, 33*

Ross, J.M. *et al.* (1972) *A Critical Appraisal of Comprehensive Education*. Slough: National Foundation for Educational Research. *74*

Runciman, W.G. (1966) *Relative Deprivation and Social Justice*. London: Routledge & Kegan Paul. *39*

Rutter, M. *et al.* (1975) Attainment and adjustment in two geographical areas. *British Journal of Psychiatry 126*: 493–533. *44*

Rutter, M. and Madge, N. (1976) *Cycles of Disadvantage: A Review of Research*. London: Heinemann. *39*

Schermerhorn, R.A. (1970) *Comparative Ethnic Relations: A Framework for Theory and Research*. New York: Random House. *85*

Schools Council (1969) *Rural Studies in Secondary Schools*. Working Paper 24. London: Evans/Methuen Educational. *32*

Schools Council (1970) *'Cross'd with Adversity': The Education of Socially Disadvantaged Children in Secondary Schools*. Working Paper 27. London: Evans/Methuen Educational. *39*

Schools Council (1975) Small schools survey (mimeo). *59, 65*

Sellman, R.R. (1968) *Devon Village Schools in the Nineteenth Century*. Newton Abbot: David & Charles. *54*

Sharp, R. (1974) The concept of cultural deprivation. Unpublished mimeo cited in J. Ahier and M. Flude (eds) *Educability, Schools and Ideology*. London: Croom Helm. *39*

Sher, J. (1977) (ed.) *Education in Rural America: A Reassessment of Conventional Wisdom*. Boulder, Colo.: Westview Press. *102*

Smith, T.L. and Zopf, P.E. (1970) *Principles of Inductive Rural Sociology*. Philadelphia: F.A. Davies. *13, 14, 15*

Solstad, K.J. (1975) School size and school transportation – some findings related to the question of the centralisation of schools in rural areas. Interskola Report. Bangor: Normal College of Education. *108*

Sorokin, P. and Zimmerman, C.C. (1929) *Principles of Rural–Urban*

Sociology. New York: Holt, Rinehart & Winston. *13*

Starr, W.E. (1978) Educational outreach: teaching by two-way radio. *Post Primary Teachers Association Journal*, July. *115*

Stephens, M. (1976) *Linguistic Minorities in Western Europe*. Dinbych: Gwasg Gomer. *87*

Stolen, A. (1975) Provision of specialist information services for teachers in large rural areas in Möre and Romsdal. Interskola Report. Bangor: Normal College of Education. *110*

Stubbs, M. (1976) *Language, Schools and Classrooms*. London: Methuen. *39*

Synge, J. (1975) The selective function and British rural education. *British Journal of Educational Studies 23*, 2: 135–52. *26*

Tonnies, F. (1957) *Community and Society*. New York: Harper Torchbooks. *14, 17*

Warner, W. Ll. *et al*. (1963) *Yankee City*. New Haven, Conn.: Yale University Press. *13*

Wax, M.L. and Wax, R.H. (1964) Formal education in an American Indian community. *Social Problems Monographs* No. 2. *39*

Welsh Education Office (1976) *Ysgol Y Dderi: An Area School in Dyfed*. Design Study No. 2. Cardiff: HMSO. *61*

Welsh Education Office (1978) *Welsh in the Schools of Gwynedd, Powys and Dyfed*. Cardiff: HMSO. *93*

Welsh Office (1964) *Depopulation in Mid-Wales*. Cardiff: HMSO. *139*

Wesolowski, W. (1978) *Classes, Strata and Power*. London: Routledge & Kegan Paul. *136*

Williams, G. (ed.) (1978) *Social and Cultural Change in Contemporary Wales*. London: Routledge & Kegan Paul. *86*

Williams, R. (1973) *The Country and the City*. London: Chatto & Windus. *136, 148*

Wirth, L. (1954) The problems of minority groups. In R. Lipton (ed.) *The Science of Man in the World Crisis*. New York: Columbia University Press. *87*

Woodruffe, B.J. (1976) *Rural Settlement Policies and Plans*. London: Oxford University Press. *146*

Yancey, W.L. *et al*. (1976) Emergent ethnicity: a review and a reformulation. *American Sociological Review 41*: 391–403. *87*

Young, I.V. (1968) *Farm Studies in Schools*. London: Association of Agriculture. *34*

Young, M.D. and Willmott, P. (1962) *Family and Kinship in East London*. Harmondsworth: Penguin. *16*

158

Subject index